THE
CHRISTMAS
COOKIE BOOK

THE CHRISTMAS COOKIE BOOK

JUDY KNIPE & BARBARA MARKS

BALLANTINE BOOKS · NEW YORK

A Ballantine Book
Published by The Ballantine Publishing Group

Copyright © 1990 by Judy Knipe and Barbara Marks
Illustrations copyright © 1990 by Patti Hefner

www.randomhouse.com/BB/

Library of Congress Cataloging-in-Publication Data
Knipe, Judy.
   The Christmas cookie book / Judy Knipe & Barbara Marks.—1st Ballantine Books ed.
      p.   cm.
   Includes index.
   ISBN 0-345-44210-5
   1. Cookies. I. Marks, Barbara. II. Title.

TX772 .K65 2000
641.8'654—dc21

                                                                    00-040366

DESIGNED BY BARBARA MARKS
ILLUSTRATIONS BY PATTI HEFNER

Manufactured in the United States of America

First Fawcett Edition: November 1990
First Ballantine Books Edition: November 2000

10 9 8 7 6 5 4 3 2

With weights and measures just and true,

Oven of even heat,

Well buttered tins, and quiet nerves,

Success will be complete.

—Epigraph for "Cookies and Crullers"
chapter of *Branford Cookbook*

❧ ACKNOWLEDGMENTS ❧

From the moment we began telling people that we were writing a Christmas cookie book, recipes were offered without stint. Friends put us in touch with other friends, and for all their help and good wishes we are truly grateful. The origins of recipes, as far as we can trace them, interest us, and many sources have been acknowledged in the recipes themselves. Thanks again to all those who helped in our search for the best: Jackie Montgomery, Rosemarie Garipoli, Nika Hazelton, Renata Rutledge, Holly Hopkins-Stamler, Nancy Inglis, Mary Garrity, Charlotte Katelvero, Claire Baksa, Joan Vass, Millie Hoffman.

Thanks also to our agents Betsy Nolan and Carla Glasser, and to our editors Ginny Faber and Joëlle Delbourgo.

We're often asked, "Who gets to eat all the cookies you've been testing?" Cookie tasters, those unsung heroes of the trenches, deserve credit, too. So thanks to Allan and Jackie; Chris, John, and Ross; Syd and Brad and Bobbie; Tesse; Susie; Pam; Janet; Gordon and Shelley; Tim and Lennie; Holly and Paul; all of the Brownie Tasters; Lynne and Ron; Nancy; Bob and Adrianne; Jeff; Peggy and Paul; Autumn and Andrew; and to Paul, who ate everything we gave him, even if it wasn't always chocolate.

Our most special thanks go to Barbara's family: Aunt Joyce Marks, Aunt Ethel McElwee, and sister Peggy Eckenbrecht for remembering and sharing family recipes and for encouragement; and most of all to Barbara's mom, Adrianne Marks, for all of the above, but especially for being the kind of mother who welcomed children in the kitchen and taught that it's always best to make things from scratch.

Blessings, too, on Janet Gilbert, Judy's friend and neighbor in Vermont, who generously gave us her mother Lepha Gilbert's heirloom recipe collection. Mrs. Gilbert was deservedly famous for her Christmas cookies, and it was exciting to read through her wonderful recipes. Some of them were carefully written up on index cards, with full instructions for mixing and baking; others were scribbled on the backs of envelopes and consisted merely of ingredients lists and cryptic notations such as "enough flour to roll out." Along with recipes from Barbara's family and the cookies we both developed specially for this book, the Gilbert recipes form the bedrock of *The Christmas Cookie Book*.

CONTENTS

Is there anyone who can resist Christmas cookies? From the homeliest fudge cookies to the most sophisticated vanilla crescents, there's something about Christmas cookies . . . they're always exactly the right size, they look so appealing, they taste so delicious; they're satisfying but not too filling.

This book is written in the belief that baking Christmas cookies should not be a chore. Many of our recipes are easy to make, and some can even be prepared in stages, using basic ingredients you have on hand. Indeed, when it comes to Christmas cookies, making them can be almost as much fun as giving them, especially if you divide up the work among several people, including children—your own or borrowed. And remember, if time and space are limited, you needn't spend days in the kitchen cranking out dozens of different types of cookies (not that we'd discourage you from doing that). A single batch of icebox cookies arranged handsomely on a platter can be an elegant and delectable treat to offer guests or to bring to a holiday gathering.

For many of us, baking Christmas cookies is among the happiest of our childhood memories, calling up the aromas and flavors of that festive season and reminding us of pleasures shared with friends and with other family members. If your youth didn't include the baking of Christmas cookies, why not create a tradition for your family and begin making and giving them this year?

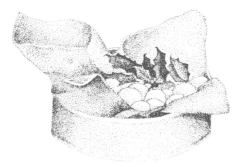

THE
CHRISTMAS
COOKIE BOOK

BEFORE YOU BEGIN TO BAKE

◦ INGREDIENTS ◦

The basic cookie ingredients are very likely on your refrigerator and pantry shelves right now: unsalted butter, large eggs, granulated sugar, brown sugar, and confectioners' sugar, all-purpose flour, baking powder, baking soda, salt, spices, and vanilla.

Most other ingredients are available at supermarkets, though a few may require a trip to a health food store. As a last resort, for items your supermarket may not carry, such as vanilla beans and imported bitter-sweet chocolate, you can go to a gourmet food shop or order by mail.

It's crucial that all your ingredients be fresh. Any food containing oil that has gone rancid not only tastes and smells awful, it's unhealthy. Don't be tempted to use that orphan stick of butter you mislaid months ago in the back of the cheese bin; throw it out. Taste and smell any nuts and flaked or shredded coconut you're planning to use before you start making the dough. Ground spices in containers that have been open for longer than six months have lost their potency; don't use them.

FLOUR We used unbleached all-purpose flour in testing most of the recipes. Any all-purpose flour will be satisfactory. If the flour measurement is for presifted flour, it will read: "2 cups sifted all-purpose flour." In all other cases, the flour was scooped out of the canister into a metal measuring cup and the excess flour leveled off with an icing spatula.

The cake flour called for in some of the recipes is *not* self-rising.

SUGAR When light or dark brown sugar is called for, you should pack it firmly into the measuring cup to measure it correctly. Confectioners' sugar need not be sifted before measuring unless the recipe so specifies. A few recipes require superfine granulated sugar; otherwise, use regular granulated sugar.

BUTTER Butter is always unsalted.

NUTS Nuts are interchangeable in many of the recipes, although certain nuts traditionally have been associated with particular cookies. Use your own good judgment about substitutions; most of them will work out very well. When grinding nuts in the food processor, add a tablespoon of sugar to prevent the nuts from turning into an oily paste. For most recipes, we chopped the nuts by hand in a wooden bowl with an old-fashioned metal chopper, since the nuts tend to exude less oil that way. But if you're in a hurry, don't hesitate to use a food processor, especially if you're chopping large quantities.

DRIED FRUITS

Dried fruits can be chopped in the food processor. To keep the pieces separated, add a bit of the flour or granulated sugar from the amount specified in the recipe. We do not recommend using prechopped packaged dates; they contain far too much sugar.

CANDIED FRUITS

It's a sad fact that the only candied fruit readily available to the home baker looks garish and tastes chemically hyperactive, so although red and green cherries are part of Christmas cookie tradition, we do not include them in our recipes. We do, however, use homemade candied citrus peel (page 120) as an ingredient. Crystallized ginger also appears in several recipes. When you buy it loose in health food stores or in Asian markets, be sure that it's still soft enough to chew. Once it has hardened, the ginger is difficult to chop.

CHOCOLATE

Use the kind that's specified in the recipe. Some of our recipes call for bar or block chocolate to be cut into pieces. To make this potentially messy task as tidy as possible, work on a large cutting board, otherwise chocolate shards will spread all over your counter. Use a heavy chef's knife and make deliberate cuts, one at a time. (Do not *chop* the chocolate as this will only shatter it.)

EQUIPMENT

BAKING SHEETS

Aside from your oven, baking sheets are the most important equipment for cookie making. We recommend using CushionAire baking sheets because they reliably produced the most evenly baked cookies we ever made. Each baking sheet (we used the 14 × 16-inch pans, but they come in smaller sizes) is made up of two baking sheets separated by a cushion of air, which prevents the cookies from overbrowning. The CushionAire sheets bake a few minutes slower than regular ones, so add a few minutes to the baking times given in our recipes if you bake with CushionAire rather than regular cookie sheets.

ELECTRIC MIXER

Of course it's possible to make a lot of these recipes without a mixer, but it's unlikely that you'd do so. While a handheld model is fine for many tasks, the sturdier mixer on a stand handles heavy doughs easily and frees your hands for other chores.

FOOD PROCESSOR

Some of our doughs are mixed in a large food processor, but an electric mixer would work just as well. A mini-processor is very useful for chopping dried fruit, nuts, and citrus rind.

KITCHEN SCALE

You will need a scale accurate in ounces to measure many ingredients such as chocolate, dried or crystallized fruits, some nuts, and the like. A scale is a good investment in any case and you'll find countless occasions to use it.

PARCHMENT PAPER

A paean of praise to parchment paper, which takes a lot of the mess out of cookie baking and spares you much time buttering and washing cookie sheets. The paper can be used several times and on both sides. You can buy parchment paper in all kitchenware shops and in any department store with a housewares section.

ICING SPATULAS

Sometimes it's the little things that make a difference in whether you enjoy your work. A small icing spatula performs a number of functions, just a few of which will give you an idea of how indispensable it is. You can use the spatula to sweep excess flour and sugar from the tops of measuring cups, scrape up the last bit of butter from its foil wrapper, clean dough off the rubber spatula with which you've scraped down your mixing bowl, dislodge cutout cookies from the scraps and transfer them to cookie sheets, and lift up the first few fragile squares from a pan of bar cookies. A large icing spatula is excellent for transferring baked cookies to racks.

TIMER

The kind of timer that keeps on ringing if you don't turn it off is best.

OVEN THERMOMETER

Use an oven thermometer because it's important to know how accurate your oven is and where the "hot spots" are.

TECHNIQUE

With a few exceptions, most of our recipes follow a standard pattern:

1. The dry ingredients are measured and combined.
2. The shortening and sugar are creamed, and eggs and flavorings added.
3. The dry ingredients are added to the creamed ones to form a dough.
4. The dough is shaped into individual cookies and sometimes deco-

rated, except for bar cookies, which are baked and then cut into individual pieces.

5. The cookies are baked and cooled, and sometimes decorated.

Special techniques as they apply to a particular category of cookie are discussed in the introductions to those categories.

We *always* rotate the cookie sheets halfway through baking, and we strongly recommend that you do, too. It's a good way to ensure that the cookies bake as evenly as possible, to monitor the baking progress of your cookies, and to see if they are baking on schedule. Our final words of advice are to remember that you must add a few minutes to the baking times given in our recipes if you bake with CushionAire rather than regular cookie sheets.

STORAGE

Food storage bags, plastic freezer containers, tins, and jars are all good cookie containers. Fragile cookies need the protection of a rigid container. Be sure your cookies have cooled completely and that the icing has set before you pack them. Cookies with decorative icing, any kind of sugar coating, or with jam filling should be packed with a sheet of wax paper between each layer.

Once they're packed in airtight containers, most cookies keep well in the refrigerator or a cool pantry for one week or more. Many cookies freeze very well, but once they are defrosted, they should be served within a few days.

And now, on to the recipes!

DROP COOKIES

Drop cookies are the least demanding of all cookies. All you have to remember is to leave enough space between cookies so that they don't meld into one huge cookie as large as the state of California. Of course, you may want a cookie that large, and certainly all kids will want one, so follow your heart in this matter.

Parchment paper is indispensable in baking drop cookies, and fortunately it can be reused on both sides.

LACE COOKIES

55 TO 60 COOKIES

1 cup chopped walnuts or pecans
1 cup all-purpose flour
½ cup light or dark corn syrup
⅔ cup packed dark brown sugar
½ stick (4 tablespoons) unsalted
    butter
¼ cup vegetable shortening

COOKIE SAMPLER

The alchemy of baking transforms the merest teaspoonful of batter into a huge, crisp, lacy wafer with a caramel-candy flavor. Although these cookies are very easy to make, they are adversely affected by humidity, so don't bake them on a damp day. The cookies are large and brittle, and if you're planning to give them away, wrap them around a rolling pin or the handle of a wooden spoon to shape them into *tuiles* as soon as they're baked, otherwise they'll be quite difficult to pack and transport. Inevitably, a few of these cookies will break; any pieces too small to serve as cookies will do admirably as topping for ice cream. A word of caution: *Do not use parchment* on the cookie sheets because it prevents the cookies from spreading as far as they can.

Preheat the oven to 325° F. Butter cookie sheets.

Spread the nuts in a pie plate and toast them in the preheated oven for 12 to 15 minutes, stirring once or twice, until they are very lightly browned and aromatic. Transfer the nuts to a bowl and let them cool. Stir in the flour and set aside. Leave the oven on.

Combine the corn syrup, sugar, butter, and shortening in a medium saucepan and place over moderate heat. Bring the mixture just to the boiling point and remove from the heat. Immediately begin beating in the flour and nut mixture until it is all incorporated.

Drop measuring teaspoons of the batter onto the cookie sheets, leaving a generous 3 inches between each cookie. Bake in the middle of the oven for 8 to 10 minutes, or until the surface of the cookies is pitted and browned. Let the cookies cool on the pan for 1 minute, then transfer to racks to cool completely. If you prefer to mold the cookies into *tuiles*, just after removing them from the pan, press them around a rolling pin or wrap them over the handle of a wooden spoon and leave until hard. Store for up to 10 days in an airtight container.

CHOCOLATE PECAN BROWNIE KISSES

36 KISSES

■

12 ounces semisweet chocolate
  (preferably imported)
2 egg whites, at room temperature
Pinch of salt
½ teaspoon white vinegar
½ teaspoon vanilla extract
½ cup superfine granulated sugar
¾ cup pecans, coarsely chopped

COOKIE SAMPLER

■

Rich, moist, chewy, chocolatey—these kisses are truly chocolate decadence. We can't think of a better way to use up 2 egg whites!

Preheat the oven to 350° F. Line cookie sheets with parchment paper or butter them.

In the top of a double boiler set over hot water, melt 6 ounces of the chocolate and let it cool. Coarsely chop the remaining 6 ounces of chocolate and set aside.

In a large bowl with an electric mixer, whip the egg whites with salt, vinegar, and vanilla until soft peaks form. Gradually add the sugar and continue beating until stiff peaks form. Fold in the cooled melted chocolate, then fold in the nuts and chopped chocolate. The batter will be very sticky.

Use your fingers or a teaspoon to drop small gobs of batter about 1½ inches apart on the prepared cookie sheets. Bake in the middle of the oven for 8 to 10 minutes, or until the cookies lose their wet look. Let them rest on the cookie sheets for 1 or 2 minutes before transferring them to wire racks to cool. Store in airtight containers in the refrigerator for up to 5 days.

MOTHER GILBERT'S HERMITS

1½ cups chopped walnuts
3 cups all-purpose flour
1½ teaspoons baking soda
1 teaspoon cinnamon
¾ teaspoon ground cloves
¾ teaspoon freshly grated nutmeg
2 sticks (1 cup) unsalted butter,
  softened
1½ cups packed brown sugar
2 large eggs
½ cup unsulfured molasses
1 cup sour milk (1 cup milk
  combined with 1 tablespoon
  fresh lemon juice or white
  vinegar), or buttermilk
1 cup golden raisins

A chewy, moist cookie, and very tasty, too. Like most hermits, this one tastes better a few days after it's been baked. Hermits can be stored in an airtight container for up to two months in a cool pantry. In fact, they keep so well that sailors used to take them on their long voyages.

Preheat the oven to 350° F. Line cookie sheets with parchment paper or butter them.

Place the walnuts in a pie plate and toast them in the preheated oven for about 8 minutes, or until they are aromatic and slightly browned. Set aside. Leave the oven on.

Combine the flour, baking soda, cinnamon, cloves, and nutmeg on a sheet of wax paper and set aside. In a large mixing bowl, cream the butter until light with an electric mixer, add the brown sugar, and beat until very well combined. Beat in the eggs, one at a time, then beat in the molasses. Add the flour mixture and sour milk alternately in thirds to the creamed mixture, beating after each addition until the batter is smooth. Fold in the raisins and toasted walnuts.

Drop scant tablespoons of the batter onto the prepared cookie sheets, leaving at least 2 inches between the cookies. Bake in the middle of the oven for about 10 minutes, or until dark golden brown. Allow the cookies to cool for 2 or 3 minutes before transferring them to racks to cool completely. Store in airtight containers for up to 2 months.

GINGERED HERMITS

2 cups all-purpose flour
1 teaspoon baking soda
2½ teaspoons ground ginger
½ teaspoon cinnamon
¼ teaspoon salt
2 sticks (1 cup) unsalted butter,
    softened
1½ cups packed dark or light
    brown sugar
3 large eggs
⅓ cup sour milk (⅓ cup milk
    combined with 1 teaspoon
    fresh lemon juice or white
    vinegar), or buttermilk
4 ounces crystallized ginger, finely
    chopped
1 generous cup sliced unblanched
    almonds
Lemon Glaze (page 116), optional

This is a homey-looking cookie, chewy and cakelike, with a delicate winy, buttery flavor.

Preheat the oven to 350° F. Line cookie sheets with parchment paper or butter them.

Combine the flour, baking soda, ground ginger, cinnamon, and salt on a piece of wax paper and set aside. In a large bowl, cream the butter until light with an electric mixer, add the brown sugar, and beat until well combined. Beat in the eggs, one at a time. Add the flour mixture and sour milk alternately in thirds to the creamed mixture, beating until the batter is smooth. Stir in the crystallized ginger and sliced almonds.

Drop teaspoonfuls of the batter on the prepared cookie sheets, leaving 2 inches between each cookie. Bake for 8 to 10 minutes, or until the cookies are medium golden brown. Slide the parchment paper off the cookie sheet and allow the cookies to set for 2 to 3 minutes before transferring them to racks to cool completely. If you baked the cookies on greased sheets, allow them to firm up for a few minutes before transferring to racks. If you wish, drizzle lemon glaze in a zigzag pattern over the surface of the cookies. Store in an airtight container for up to 2 weeks or freeze for up to 2 months.

ORANGE MINCEMEAT COOKIES

60 TO 65 COOKIES

1¾ cups all-purpose flour
¼ teaspoon salt
1½ teaspoons baking soda
½ teaspoon cinnamon
½ teaspoon ground ginger
½ teaspoon freshly grated nutmeg
¼ cup granulated sugar
2 oranges
1½ sticks (¾ cup) unsalted butter,
    softened
⅓ cup packed dark brown sugar
1 large egg
1 teaspoon vanilla extract
6 ounces condensed mincemeat,
    crumbled (1 cup, packed)
¾ cup chopped walnuts
¼ cup chopped Candied Orange
    Peel (page 120), optional

These soft, subtly spiced cookies keep very well for a couple of weeks stored at room temperature. They cry out for a glass of milk.

Preheat the oven to 350° F. Line cookie sheets with parchment paper or butter them.

Combine the flour, salt, baking soda, and spices on a piece of wax paper and set aside. Place the granulated sugar in the bowl of a food processor (preferably a mini-processor) fitted with the steel blade. With a citrus zester, remove the zest from the oranges, allowing the strips to fall into the processor bowl. Process the sugar and zest until the zest is grated, about 1 minute. Reserve. Squeeze the oranges, strain the juice, and set aside 7 tablespoons, reserving the remaining juice for another use.

In a mixing bowl, cream the butter with an electric mixer. Add the orange zest mixture and the brown sugar and beat until light and fluffy. Add the egg and vanilla and beat well. Alternately add the flour mixture and the 7 tablespoons of orange juice, beating well after each addition until the batter is smooth. Fold in the mincemeat, walnuts, and candied orange peel, if desired.

Drop the batter by teaspoonfuls onto the prepared cookie sheets, leaving 2 inches between each cookie. Bake for 8 to 10 minutes, or until golden brown. Transfer the cookies to racks to cool completely. Store in airtight containers for up to 2 weeks, or freeze for up to 2 months.

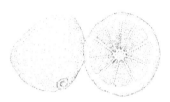

Aunt Hattie's Lemon Cream Cookies

70 TO 75 COOKIES

■

½ cup slivered blanched almonds
½ cup granulated sugar
2 lemons
½ cup packed dark brown sugar
2 large eggs
1 cup heavy cream
2 cups all-purpose flour
½ teaspoon salt
1 teaspoon baking soda

"Aunt Hattie's Cream Cookies (modified)" is the title of this recipe as it appears on one of Mrs. Gilbert's index cards, with this comment at the end of the ingredients list: "They should drop like maple candy!" And so they do! A food processor, a citrus zester, and a few measuring implements are all you'll need to produce tender, golden cookies with a cakelike texture and a clear lemon flavor. Eat them within a day or two of baking, or freeze them for later giving.

Preheat the oven to 350° F. Line cookie sheets with parchment paper or butter them.

Place the almonds on a baking sheet or pie plate and toast them in the preheated oven for about 4 minutes, or just until they are crisp and very faintly colored. Set the almonds aside to cool. Leave the oven on.

Place granulated sugar in the bowl of a food processor fitted with the steel blade. Remove the zest from the lemons with a citrus zester, allowing the strips of zest to fall into the processor bowl. (Reserve the lemons for another use.) Process the zest and sugar until the zest is grated, about 1 minute. Add the brown sugar, eggs, and cream, and process until very well mixed, 30 to 45 seconds. Sprinkle in the flour, salt, and baking soda and process until the batter is thick and very smooth, 30 to 45 seconds.

Drop rounded teaspoonfuls of the batter on the prepared cookie sheets, leaving 1½ inches between cookies, then sprinkle the top of each cookie with 2 or 3 pieces of toasted slivered almonds. Bake in the center of the oven for 8 to 10 minutes, or until the cookies are golden brown. Transfer the cookies to racks to cool. Store in airtight containers for up to 3 days; the cookies can be frozen for up to 2 months.

COOKIE SAMPLER
■

ORANGE MINCEMEAT
COOKIES
page 16

MORAVIAN
MOLASSES COOKIES
page 105

BUTTERSCOTCH
COOKIES
page 65

AMY'S MOLASSES PUFFS

40 TO 45 COOKIES

2 cups all-purpose flour
1 teaspoon baking soda
¼ teaspoon salt
½ cup vegetable shortening
⅓ cup packed dark brown sugar
1 large egg
½ cup unsulfured molasses
¼ cup brewed coffee
Sliced natural almonds

COOKIE SAMPLER

This simplest of recipes bakes up into light, soft, tasty cookies. The combination of coffee and molasses deepens the flavor.

Preheat the oven to 375° F. Line cookie sheets with parchment paper or grease them.

On a sheet of wax paper, combine the flour, baking soda, and salt. In a mixing bowl, cream the shortening with an electric mixer, add the brown sugar, and beat until well mixed. Beat in the egg, molasses, and coffee. Add the flour mixture and beat until smooth.

Drop the dough by heaping teaspoonfuls on the prepared cookie sheets, leaving about 1½ inches between each, and stick a few almond slices upright into the top of each cookie. Bake in the middle of the oven for 10 to 12 minutes, or until golden around the edges. Transfer to racks to cool. Store in an airtight container for up to 2 weeks, or freeze for up to 2 months.

OLD-FASHIONED FUDGE COOKIES

50 TO 55 COOKIES

1½ cups all-purpose flour
1 teaspoon baking soda
¼ teaspoon salt
1 stick (½ cup) unsalted butter,
  softened
1 cup packed dark brown sugar
1 large egg
2 squares unsweetened chocolate,
  melted
1 teaspoon vanilla extract
½ cup raisins or chopped dates
½ cup chopped walnuts or pecans

Easy to make, with a straightforward chocolate flavor, the recipe for this beloved cookie jar treat was given to us by Janet Gilbert.

Preheat the oven to 350° F. Line cookie sheets with parchment paper or butter them.

On a piece of wax paper, combine the flour, baking soda, and salt, and set aside. In a large bowl, cream the butter until light with an electric mixer, add the brown sugar, and continue beating until the mixture is fluffy. Beat in the egg, then add the melted chocolate and vanilla and beat until well mixed. Add the flour mixture and beat until smooth. Fold in the raisins and nuts.

Drop the dough by teaspoonfuls onto the prepared sheets, leaving 1½ inches between cookies, or mold the dough into 1-inch balls. Bake in the middle of the oven for 8 to 10 minutes for chewy cookies or for about 12 minutes for crisp ones. Transfer to racks to cool completely. Store in airtight containers for up to 1 week; freeze for up to 2 months.

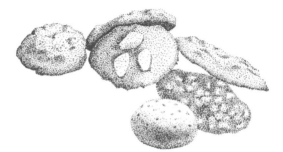

OAT DROP CAKES

55 TO 60 COOKIES

1⅛ cups rye flour
1¼ cups old-fashioned rolled oats
2 teaspoons baking powder
½ teaspoon salt
1 teaspoon cinnamon
¼ cup vegetable shortening
½ stick (¼ cup) unsalted butter,
    softened
¼ cup packed dark brown sugar
½ cup dark or light corn syrup
1 large egg
3 tablespoons water
¾ cup dark raisins
¾ cup coarsely chopped walnuts

Rye flour gives these old-fashioned cookies an earthy flavor. Because the dough is fairly indestructible and stiff enough to drop on the cookie sheets by hand, you can round up a child or two as kitchen help.

Preheat the oven to 350° F. Line cookie sheets with parchment paper or butter them.

On a piece of wax paper, combine the rye flour, rolled oats, baking powder, salt, and cinnamon. In a large mixing bowl, cream the shortening and butter with an electric mixer. Add the brown sugar and continue beating until the mixture is very well mixed. Beat in the corn syrup, egg, and water. Add the rolled oats mixture in thirds to the creamed mixture, beating well. Stir in the raisins and nuts.

Drop the dough on the cookie sheets by tablespoonfuls, leaving 2 inches between each cookie, and bake in the middle of the oven for 10 to 12 minutes, or until the edges are barely golden brown. Transfer the cookies to racks to cool completely before storing in an airtight container, where they will last for at least 1 week or up to 2 months in the freezer.

OATMEAL CURRANT COOKIES

ABOUT 60 COOKIES

▪

2 cups all-purpose flour
½ teaspoon salt
½ teaspoon baking powder
1 teaspoon baking soda
½ teaspoon cinnamon
2 sticks (1 cup) unsalted butter,
    softened
1¼ cups granulated sugar
1 cup packed light brown sugar
2 large eggs
1 teaspoon grated lemon or
    orange zest
2 cups old-fashioned rolled oats
1 cup walnuts, chopped
½ cup dried currants

Sweet, cinnamony, and fragrant, just what a good oatmeal cookie should be. These spread during baking, making a thin, crisp, crunchy cookie. For a cookie that is more rounded and keeps its shape, refrigerate the dough for an hour or two before dropping onto cookie sheets.

Preheat the oven to 350° F. Line cookie sheets with parchment paper or butter them.

On a piece of wax paper, combine the flour, salt, baking powder, baking soda, and cinnamon. In a large bowl with an electric mixer, cream the butter and sugars until light and fluffy. Add the eggs one at a time, beating well after each addition. Add the flour mixture, beating until smooth, then stir in the grated rind, rolled oats, walnuts, and currants.

Drop rounded teaspoonfuls of the dough 1½ inches apart on the prepared sheets. Bake in the middle of the oven for 13 minutes, or until lightly browned. Let the cookies cool slightly on the baking sheets before transferring to wire racks to cool completely. The cookies will puff up during baking and then will fall as they cool. Store in airtight containers for up to 1 week or in the freezer for up to 2 months.

VARIATION   Substitute chopped dried apricots for the currants.

21

CRANBERRY COOKIES

50 TO 60 COOKIES

•

1 ¼ cups sifted all-purpose flour
½ teaspoon baking soda
¼ teaspoon salt
½ stick (¼ cup) unsalted butter,
    softened
¼ cup vegetable shortening
6 tablespoons granulated sugar
6 tablespoons light brown sugar
1 large egg
½ teaspoon vanilla extract
1 cup raw cranberries, chopped
½ cup chopped Candied Orange
    and Lemon Peel (page 120)
½ cup chopped walnuts or pecans

For a chewier cookie, substitute ¾ cup of dark brown sugar for the granulated and light brown sugars and bake the cookies 2 or 3 minutes less than directed in the recipe. If good-quality candied citrus peel is not available, don't use the gummy, flavorless kind to be found in most supermarkets; instead, substitute the finely grated zest of 1 large orange.

Combine the flour, baking soda, and salt on a sheet of wax paper and set aside. In a large bowl with an electric mixer, cream the butter and shortening until light. Add the sugars and beat until fluffy. Add the egg and beat well, then beat in the vanilla. Add the flour mixture and stir until well combined. Add the cranberries, candied peel, and nuts, and stir until thoroughly incorporated. Cover the dough with wax paper and refrigerate for 1 hour, or until firm.

Preheat the oven to 375° F. Line baking sheets with parchment paper or butter them.

Drop the dough by teaspoonfuls onto the prepared cookie sheets, leaving 1½ inches between each cookie. Bake the cookies in the middle of the oven for 9 to 11 minutes, or until they are golden. Leave on the cookie sheets for 2 or 3 minutes, then transfer to racks to cool. Store the cookies in airtight containers for up to 1 week; freeze for up to 2 months.

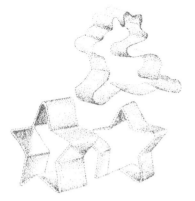

CHOCOLATE COCONUT PECAN COOKIES

ABOUT 60 COOKIES

∎

1 cup all-purpose flour
1 teaspoon baking powder
¼ teaspoon salt
1 stick (½ cup) unsalted butter, softened
1 cup granulated sugar
2 large eggs
½ teaspoon vanilla extract
2 ounces unsweetened chocolate, melted
1 cup flaked coconut
½ cup pecans, chopped
¾ cup semisweet chocolate chips
About 60 pecan halves

Their plain appearance belies the delicious flavor of these crisp, chocolatey cookies. If you like a chewier cookie, chill the dough for an hour or two before dropping it; that way the cookies won't spread as much during baking, and the centers will stay moist.

Preheat the oven to 350° F. Line cookie sheets with parchment paper or butter them.

On a piece of wax paper, combine the flour, baking powder, and salt. In a large bowl, cream the butter with an electric mixer, add the sugar, and beat until fluffy. Beat in the eggs and vanilla, then add the melted chocolate and beat well. Add the flour mixture, mixing until smooth, then stir in the coconut, chopped pecans, and chocolate chips.

Drop the dough from a teaspoon onto the prepared cookie sheets, leaving about 2 inches between each cookie. Press a pecan half on top of each cookie. Bake in the middle of the oven for 10 to 13 minutes, or until set. Transfer cookies to wire racks to cool. Store in airtight containers for up to 1 week or in the freezer for up to 2 months.

COOKIE SAMPLER

∎

ANISE DROPS

ABOUT 30 COOKIES

▪

1⅓ cups all-purpose flour
¾ teaspoon baking powder
1 tablespoon aniseed
⅔ stick (⅓ cup) unsalted butter, softened
½ cup granulated sugar
2 large eggs
½ teaspoon vanilla extract

These pale, beautifully mounded cookies come from the files of Rosemarie Garipoli. A form of biscotti, they are wonderfully aromatic with a delicate touch of aniseed. Somewhat cakelike in texture, they are delicious served with espresso or a glass of Sambuca. The cookies will develop their fullest flavor if left overnight.

Preheat the oven to 350° F. Line cookie sheets with parchment paper or butter them.

On a sheet of wax paper combine the flour, baking powder, and aniseed. In a mixing bowl, cream the butter and sugar with an electric mixer until light and fluffy. Add the eggs, one at a time, beating well after each addition, then beat in the vanilla. Add the flour mixture and beat until the dough is smooth.

Drop by heaping teaspoonfuls onto the prepared sheets, leaving 1½ inches between each cookie. Bake in the middle of the oven for 8 to 10 minutes, or until the edges of the cookies have barely begun to color. Transfer to racks to cool. Store in airtight containers for up to 1 week.

For smaller (and more) cookies, drop the dough by scant teaspoonfuls and bake for 5 to 8 minutes.

COOKIE SAMPLER

▪

OATMEAL WAFERS
page 37

SHORTBREAD
page 93

ANISE DROPS
page 24

MOLDED COOKIES

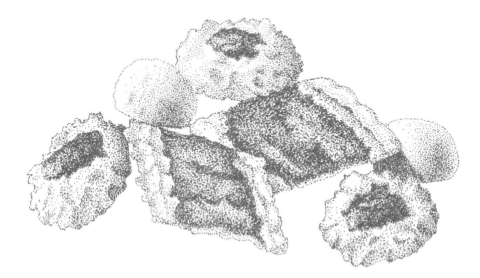

We love making molded cookies, which is why we've included so many recipes for them.

Molded cookies offer one great advantage, aside from flavor—the most important reason for making any cookie. Once they are shaped, most of these cookies can be frozen on baking sheets and then transferred to freezer bags and stored for several months before baking. And of course, you don't have to bake them all at once. If you decide to follow this course with any of the recipes, add 3 or 4 minutes to the baking time given.

RENATA'S VANILLA CRESCENTS

*1 cup (about 6 ounces)
    unblanched almonds*
½ cup granulated sugar
2 cups sifted all-purpose flour
Pinch of salt
*2 sticks (1 cup) unsalted butter,
    cut into 12 to 16 pieces and
    softened*
*Juice and grated zest of ½ small
    lemon*
1 teaspoon vanilla extract
*Vanilla Confectioners' Sugar
    (page 119) or sifted
    confectioners' sugar, for
    dusting*
*Chocolate Dipping Glaze
    (optional; page 118)*

Elegant and rich but not cloyingly sweet, these cookies are a traditional Viennese Christmas treat. They are very fragile during and just after baking, so handle them carefully when you rotate the baking sheets, and transfer the baked cookies to racks gently. The snowy white crescents look spectacular arranged on a dark platter or tray, and they make a good light dessert after a heavy meal.

Place the almonds and 2 tablespoons of the granulated sugar in the bowl of a food processor fitted with the steel blade and process until the almonds are ground, about 1 minute. Add the remaining sugar, flour, and salt and pulse the mixture 3 or 4 times until the ingredients are well mixed. Distribute the butter evenly on top of the almond mixture. Sprinkle with the lemon juice and rind and the vanilla and process until you have a smooth, soft dough. Scrape the dough out onto a piece of wax paper and form it into a ball. Wrap in wax paper and refrigerate for about 1½ hours, or until firm but not rock-hard.

Preheat the oven to 350° F. Line cookie sheets with parchment paper or butter them.

Divide the dough into quarters and cut each quarter into 14 pieces. Roll the pieces into cigar shapes about 3 inches long and tapered at the ends, then curve them into crescents. (The cookies can now be frozen for later baking, as described on page 27.) Place the cookies ¾ inch apart on the prepared cookie sheets and bake in the middle of the oven for 13 to 18 minutes, or just until golden at the edges. Cool the cookies for 2 or 3 minutes on the baking sheets, then carefully transfer to racks set over wax paper. While they are still warm, generously dust them with vanilla confectioners' sugar or plain confectioners' sugar. If you like, dip one or both tips of the cookies in chocolate glaze. Store in airtight containers at room temperature for 3 to 4 days.

JAN HAGELS (DUTCH BUTTER STRIPS)

ABOUT 33 STRIPS

2 cups all-purpose flour
1 teaspoon cinnamon
1 teaspoon ground ginger
2 sticks (1 cup) unsalted butter, softened
1 cup granulated sugar
1 large egg, separated
1 teaspoon vanilla extract
1 tablespoon water
1 to 1½ cups finely chopped walnuts or pecans

COOKIE SAMPLER

LINZER WREATHS
page 92

JAN HAGELS
page 29

PINWHEELS
page 70

**OR
MARBLE COOKIES**
page 71

Crisp and buttery, these cookies are further enhanced with spices and nuts. Cut them any size you like—we prefer long narrow fingers, but they would do nicely in squares, diamonds, or larger rectangles.

Preheat the oven to 350° F. Lightly butter a 15½ × 10½-inch jelly roll pan, or use a nonstick pan. You can also pat the dough into a free-form 16 × 11-inch rectangle on a lightly buttered or parchment-lined cookie sheet.

Combine the flour, cinnamon, and ginger on a sheet of wax paper and set aside. In a large mixing bowl, cream the butter with an electric mixer, add the sugar, and beat until light and fluffy. Beat in the egg yolk until the mixture is well combined, then beat in the vanilla. Add the flour mixture and stir until it is completely incorporated.

Turn the dough out on the prepared jelly roll pan and pat it into an even sheet. In a cup or small bowl, beat the egg white and water until frothy and brush the mixture over the dough. Sprinkle the nuts evenly over the dough and press them in lightly. Using a long ruler and a sharp knife, cut the dough into thirds lengthwise, then cut each third crosswise into strips about 1⅓ inches wide. Bake for about 20 minutes, or until the sheet is light golden brown. (If you've used a CushionAire cookie sheet to bake a free-form rectangle, the baking time may be a few minutes longer.) Place the pan on a rack and immediately cut along the original cutting marks.

Transfer the strips to racks and allow them to cool completely. Store in an airtight container for up to 2 weeks or for up to 2 months in the freezer.

PECAN BALLS

90 COOKIES

·

2 cups sifted all-purpose flour
⅛ teaspoon salt
1¼ cups pecans, hazelnuts, or
*   walnuts, or a combination of*
*   all 3, ground*
2 sticks (1 cup) unsalted butter,
*   softened*
½ cup granulated sugar
1 teaspoon vanilla extract
Cinnamon Sugar (page 120),
*   Vanilla Sugar (page 119), or*
*   Vanilla Confectioners' Sugar*
*   (page 119)*

This recipe came from Barbara's mother, Adrianne. They're plain-looking cookies, but with a sophisticated taste. You can store the frozen, unbaked balls of dough for up to 3 months in a freezer bag, then bake them whenever you like.

Combine the flour, salt, and ground nuts on a sheet of wax paper, and set aside. In a mixing bowl, cream the butter with an electric mixer, add the granulated sugar, and beat until the mixture is light and fluffy. Beat in the vanilla, then add the flour and pecan mixture and mix very well, at first with the mixer and then with your hands. The dough will be very soft; form it into a ball, wrap in wax paper, and refrigerate for 1 to 2 hours, or until firm.

Break off small pieces of dough and form them into cherry-sized balls. Place the nut balls on a baking sheet and freeze them. Either bake the cookies as soon as they are frozen, or store them in freezer bags for up to 3 months.

Preheat the oven to 350° F. Place the frozen pecan balls 1 inch apart on ungreased cookie sheets and transfer the sheets very carefully to the oven. (The frozen balls of dough skid around on the cookie sheets, and if you're not careful they can fall off and roll all over the kitchen floor.) Bake the cookies immediately in the middle of the oven for 13 to 18 minutes, or until they are barely golden at the edges. Cool on the baking sheets for 2 or 3 minutes. Pour the dusting sugar you've chosen into a flat soup bowl, roll the warm cookies in the sugar, and transfer them to racks to cool. Store in an airtight container for up to 1 week; freeze for up to 2 months.

CHOCOLATE PECAN BALLS

Increase the granulated sugar to 10 tablespoons (an addition of 2 tablespoons). Add 6 tablespoons of unsweetened cocoa powder (preferably Dutch-process cocoa) to the creamed mixture. The dough will be very stiff, so you'll

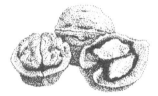

have to knead in the final addition of the flour mixture by hand. Form the dough into balls, freeze, and bake as directed. Allow the cookies to cool for 3 to 4 minutes on the baking sheet, then transfer to racks. While they are still warm, dust the cookies generously with plain or vanilla confectioners' sugar.

HOLLY'S GINGER CRISPS

48 COOKIES

2¼ cups all-purpose flour
2 teaspoons baking soda
¼ teaspoon salt
1 teaspoon ground ginger
½ teaspoon cinnamon
½ cup shortening
½ stick (¼ cup) unsalted butter, softened
1 cup granulated sugar
1 large egg
¼ cup unsulfured molasses
2 ounces crystallized ginger, minced
Granulated sugar

These crisp, spicy gingersnaps came from our friend Holly Hopkins-Stamler. The recipe has been in her family for years. They are delicious hot from the oven and even better after they've ripened—good cookies to include in a CARE package since they travel well, and their flavor only improves with time.

Preheat the oven to 350° F. Line cookie sheets with parchment paper or butter them.

On a piece of wax paper, combine the flour, baking soda, salt, ground ginger, and cinnamon. In a large bowl, cream the shortening and butter with an electric mixer, add the sugar, and beat until light and fluffy. Beat in the egg, then add the molasses and beat until smooth. Add the flour mixture, mixing well. Stir in the crystallized ginger.

Divide the dough into quarters and cut each quarter into 12 pieces. Form the pieces into 1-inch balls and place them 1 inch apart on the prepared sheets. Flatten each ball with the bottom of a glass buttered and dipped in sugar. Bake in the middle of the oven for 10 to 13 minutes, or until firm but not hard to the touch. Transfer to wire racks to cool completely. Store in airtight containers for 3 to 4 weeks. You can keep these cookies in the freezer for up to 3 months.

CHOCOLATE CRINKLES

60 TO 72 COOKIES

∙

2 cups all-purpose flour
2 teaspoons baking powder
¼ teaspoon salt
½ cup vegetable shortening
4 ounces unsweetened chocolate
2 cups granulated sugar
4 large eggs
2 teaspoons vanilla extract
Confectioners' sugar, Cinnamon
    Sugar (page 120), or
    unsweetened cocoa powder
Walnut or pecan halves

A recipe from Barbara's mom. In the original, the balls of dough are rolled in confectioners' sugar before baking. As the cookies bake, they expand, leaving dark chocolate fissures in the powdery sugar coating. Slight variations on this theme make a big difference in the appearance and flavor of the cookie. When you roll the balls of dough in cinnamon sugar, the baked cookies look like ginger snaps and taste delicious, almost harmonic, so well does the cinnamon complement the chocolate. Rolling the dough balls in unsweetened cocoa powder gives the baked cookies the appearance of a jacquard fabric—chocolate on chocolate—and, of course, a profoundly chocolate flavor.

Combine the flour, baking powder, and salt, and set aside.

In the top of a double boiler over hot but not boiling water, melt the shortening and chocolate. Transfer the mixture to a mixing bowl and, with an electric mixer, beat in the granulated sugar. Add the eggs, one at a time, beating well. Stir in the vanilla. Add the dry ingredients and mix well. Chill the dough for at least 1 hour.

Preheat the oven to 350° F. Line cookie sheets with parchment paper or butter them.

Form the dough into balls about 1 inch in diameter and roll each ball in confectioners' sugar. Place the balls about 2 inches apart on the prepared cookie sheets. Place a nut half firmly on top of each ball, flattening the ball slightly. Bake in the middle of the oven for 8 to 10 minutes, or until cookies are firm around the edges but still soft in the center. For crisper cookies, bake a little longer.

CINAMMON CHOCOLATE SNAPS

Instead of confectioners' sugar, roll the balls of dough in cinnamon sugar.

COCOA CHOCOLATE SNAPS

Instead of confectioners' sugar, roll the balls in sifted unsweetened cocoa powder.

PFEFFERNÜSSE

∎

2 large eggs
¾ cup granulated sugar
¾ cup packed dark brown sugar
3 ounces Candied Orange or
    Lemon Peel (page 120)
2 cups all-purpose flour
½ teaspoon baking soda
¼ teaspoon salt
2 teaspoons cinnamon
1 teaspoon ground cardamom
½ teaspoon freshly grated nutmeg
½ teaspoon ground allspice
½ teaspoon ground cloves
¼ teaspoon freshly ground black
    pepper
¼ cup ground blanched almonds
Grated zest of 1 lemon
Sifted confectioners' sugar or
    Armagnac Glaze (page 116)

These are the pfeffernüsse we remember, crisp and crunchy on the outside, slightly chewy on the inside. Chewy changes to crunchy after the cookies are a day or two old. Bite into a pfeffernüsse and you'll be treated to a spectrum of spices. Iced with an Armagnac glaze or dusted with powdered sugar, these are a Christmas cookie staple. After the dough has been shaped into balls, it must ripen overnight before it is baked.

Place the eggs and sugars in the bowl of a heavy-duty electric mixer and beat with the beater attachment at medium speed for 10 minutes.

Meanwhile, place the candied peel and 1 tablespoon of the flour in a small food processor and chop fine, or chop the peel by hand. Set aside. Combine the remaining flour, the baking soda, salt, cinnamon, cardamom, nutmeg, allspice, cloves, pepper, almonds, and lemon zest on a piece of wax paper. After the egg mixture has been beaten for 10 minutes, gradually add the flour mixture and beat until well mixed. Add the candied peel and continue beating until the dough cleans the side of the bowl and forms a ball.

Line cookie sheets with parchment paper or butter them. Form the dough into 1-inch balls and place them 1 inch apart on the cookie sheets. Let the balls of dough ripen overnight at room temperature.

Preheat the oven to 350° F. Bake the pfeffernüsse in the middle of the oven for 15 minutes, or until deep cracks have formed in the tops. Roll the cookies in confectioners' sugar while they are still hot, then cool thoroughly on racks. If you wish to glaze the cookies with Armagnac glaze instead, do so while they are warm. Store in airtight containers at room temperature for up to 4 weeks.

AUNT MARIE'S THIMBLE COOKIES

ABOUT **48** COOKIES

•

1¾ cups all-purpose flour
1 teaspoon baking powder
¼ teaspoon salt
¾ cup vegetable shortening
½ cup packed light brown sugar
½ cup smooth peanut butter
1 large egg
½ teaspoon orange extract
½ to ¾ cup red currant jelly

This old-time recipe came from Barbara's great-aunt, who also used this dough for plain peanut butter cookies. No one else's peanut butter cookies tasted like Aunt Marie's; her secret was orange extract.

Preheat the oven to 350° F. Line cookie sheets with parchment paper or grease them.

On a piece of wax paper, combine the flour, baking powder, and salt, and set aside. In a large bowl with an electric mixer, cream the shortening and brown sugar until light. Add the peanut butter, egg, and orange extract and beat well. Add the flour mixture and continue beating the dough until smooth.

Form the dough into 1-inch balls and place them 1½ inches apart on the prepared cookie sheets. Make thimble-sized dents in the top of each cookie as follows: Invert the closed bottle of orange extract, dip the cap into granulated sugar, then press the cap deep into the center of each ball of dough. Bake the cookies in the middle of the oven for 10 to 13 minutes, or until golden brown. Transfer the cookies to wire racks to cool. Fill as many cookies as you will be serving or giving immediately with red currant jelly. Store the filled cookies in airtight containers for up to 1 week and in the freezer for up to 2 months.

**AUNT MARIE'S
PEANUT BUTTER
COOKIES**

To make peanut butter cookies like the ones remembered from childhood, make the 1-inch balls of dough and arrange them on the cookie sheets 1½ inches apart. Press the tines of a fork into each ball, first in one direction and then in the other, to create a crisscross pattern. Keep dipping the fork in granulated sugar to prevent it from sticking to the dough. Decorate the tops of the cookies with chocolate shot or press a semisweet chocolate chip into the center of each cookie before baking. Bake the cookies in the middle of the oven for 10 to 13 minutes, or until golden brown.

Transfer the cookies to wire racks to cool. Store the cookies in airtight containers for up to 1 week and in the freezer for up to 2 months.

COOKIES BY CORNELIA

72 COOKIES

·

2 cups all-purpose flour
1½ teaspoons baking soda
¼ teaspoon salt
1 teaspoon cinnamon
½ teaspoon ground ginger
1½ sticks (¾ cup) unsalted butter, softened
1 cup granulated sugar
1 large egg
¼ cup unsulfured molasses
Cinnamon Sugar (page 120)

This recipe was passed along to us as part of Mrs. Gilbert's Christmas cookie files. Thanks, Cornelia (she was Mrs. Gilbert's hairdresser), for these uncomplicated but deliciously crisp cookies, with their slightly crackled tops and mild molasses and spice flavor. If you aren't too fussy about size and shape, you can enlist a child's help in forming the dough into balls and rolling them in sugar. The cookies are best baked on a dry day.

Preheat the oven to 350° F. Line cookie sheets with parchment paper or lightly butter them.

On a sheet of wax paper, combine the flour, baking soda, salt, cinnamon, and ginger. In a large mixing bowl, cream the butter with an electric mixer, add the sugar, and beat until fluffy. Beat in the egg and molasses. Add the dry ingredients in thirds and beat until well blended.

Divide the dough into quarters and cut each quarter into 18 pieces. Form the pieces into balls, roll them in cinnamon sugar, and place 2½ inches apart on the prepared cookie sheets. (The cookies flatten and spread out as they bake, so don't skimp on the space between them.) Bake in the middle of the oven for 8 to 10 minutes, or until the cookies are a rich brown. Transfer to racks to cool completely. Store in an airtight container for up to 4 weeks. Frozen cookies keep well, too; pack them in heavy-duty freezer bags and store for up to 3 months.

DELLAWITZES

ABOUT 175 COOKIES

■

2 pounds pitted dates
8 ounces Candied Orange or
    Lemon Peel (page 120) or a
    combination of the two
8 ounces walnuts, chopped
8 ounces almonds, chopped
8 ounces brazil nuts, chopped
4 ounces crystallized ginger,
    chopped
2½ cups all-purpose flour
1 teaspoon salt
1 teaspoon baking soda
2 sticks (1 cup) unsalted butter,
    softened
1½ cups packed light brown sugar
2 large eggs

COOKIE SAMPLER

■

DELLAWITZES
page 36

PECAN BALLS
page 30

JAN HAGELS
page 29

The family recipe for these wonderful, rich, chewy cookies was generously given to us by our friend Nancy Inglis. The recipe came to her from her husband's aunt who, when she tasted them for the first time, asked what kind of cookies they were. She was told that they were Della-witzes. It turned out that Della Witz was the *baker* of the cookies. The name stuck, however, and they have been called Dellawitzes ever since.

This recipe yields about 6½ pounds of dough—that's a lot of cookies! At times while you're molding balls of dough, you may think that it's increasing in volume every time you turn your head. Dellawitzes are perfect to make with several other people, including children.

Preheat the oven to 350° F. Line cookie sheets with parchment paper or butter them.

Using a food processor fitted with the steel blade, chop the dates, candied peel, and crystallized ginger in batches, using some of the flour to keep the pieces of fruit from sticking together. As it's chopped, transfer the fruit to a very large bowl. Add the nuts to the fruit, toss to mix, and set aside.

On a piece of wax paper, combine the remaining flour, salt, and baking soda. In the large bowl of an electric mixer, cream the butter and brown sugar until well mixed. Beat in the eggs one at a time, beating well after each ad-dition, then beat in the flour mixture. Begin adding the fruit and nut mixture as you continue to beat the dough. When the dough mass gets too large for the bowl, transfer the mixture to a huge mixing bowl and continue to incor-porate the fruit and nut mixture into the dough with your hands. It helps at this point if there's one person to hold the bowl while another mixes in the fruit and nuts. Try not to laugh too hard.

Form the dough into 1-inch balls, wetting your hands

in cold water from time to time to keep the dough from forming a gunky layer on your palms, and place the cookies 1 inch apart on the prepared sheets. Bake in the middle of the oven for 10 minutes, or until lightly browned. Transfer the cookies to wire racks to cool. Store in airtight containers for up to 2 weeks or freeze for up to 2 months.

OATMEAL WAFERS

40 TO 48 COOKIES

1½ sticks (¾ cup) unsalted butter, softened
1 teaspoon vanilla extract
¾ cup packed light or dark brown sugar
1½ cups old-fashioned rolled oats
¾ cup all-purpose flour
½ teaspoon baking soda
¼ teaspoon salt
1 tablespoon wheat germ
¾ cup chopped walnuts
Cinnamon Sugar (page 120)

Thanks to Charlotte Katelvero, here's the recipe you've always dreamed of—just a list of ingredients with instructions to simply throw them all into a bowl and beat until they're well mixed. The wafers are crisp and buttery, with a pebbly texture of oatmeal and chopped nuts.

Preheat the oven to 350° F. Line cookie sheets with parchment paper or butter them.

Place the butter, vanilla, brown sugar, oats, flour, baking soda, salt, wheat germ, and nuts in a bowl and with an electric mixer beat until very well mixed, or knead by hand until the dough is homogenous.

Divide the dough into quarters and cut each quarter into 10 to 12 pieces. Pour cinnamon sugar in a shallow soup bowl. Form the pieces of dough into balls and roll them in the cinnamon sugar. Place the cookies on the prepared sheets and flatten them with the bottom of a glass that has been buttered and dipped into the cinnamon sugar; the cookies should be a scant ¼ inch thick. Arrange the cookies about 1 inch apart on the prepared sheets and bake in the middle of the oven for 8 to 10 minutes. Cool for 2 minutes on the baking sheets, then transfer to racks to cool. Store at room temperature in an airtight container for up to 2 weeks or freeze for 2 months.

ORANGE CHOCOLATE CHUNK COOKIES

60 TO 65 COOKIES

■

1 ⅛ *cups sifted all-purpose flour*
¼ *teaspoon baking soda*
¼ *teaspoon salt*
½ *stick (¼ cup) unsalted butter,*
    softened
¼ *cup vegetable shortening*
¼ *cup granulated sugar*
¼ *cup packed light brown sugar*
1 *large egg*
1 *teaspoon vanilla extract*
8 *ounces bittersweet or semisweet*
    chocolate (preferably
    imported), not chocolate
    chips, cut into ¼- to ⅜-inch
    pieces
Generous ¾ cup chopped Candied
    Orange Peel, or Orange and
    Lemon Peel (page 120)
1 *cup coarsely chopped hazelnuts*
    or macadamia nuts

Created for lovers of chocolate chip cookies, these are liberally studded with chunks of bittersweet chocolate, nuts, and candied orange peel. They're reason enough for making your own candied citrus rinds, because the kind you buy in supermarkets simply won't do. The double chocolate variation that follows is for those who think that there can never be too much chocolate.

Combine the flour, baking soda, and salt on a piece of wax paper, and set aside. In a large mixing bowl, preferably with an electric mixer, cream the butter and shortening until light. Add the sugars and continue beating until fluffy. Add the egg and beat well, then beat in the vanilla. Add the flour mixture, beating until the dough is well mixed. Add the chocolate, chopped citrus peel, and nuts and fold in by hand or, if you have a heavy-duty mixer, until the dough cleans the sides of the bowl. The raw dough is delicious, so try not to eat it all before you bake the cookies.

Turn the dough out onto a sheet of wax paper, form it into a ball, wrap it in the wax paper, and refrigerate for 2 hours or overnight.

Preheat the oven to 375° F. Line cookie sheets with parchment paper or butter them.

Divide the chilled dough into quarters and cut each quarter into 16 pieces. Roll the pieces into 1-inch balls and place them a generous 1 inch apart on the prepared sheets. If you prefer not to bake all the cookies at once, they can be frozen for later baking (see page 27). Bake in the middle of the oven for about 9 minutes for chewy cookies or for 11 to 13 minutes for crisp ones. Store in airtight containers for up to 1 week or in the freezer for up to 2 months.

DOUBLE CHOCOLATE GINGER MACADAMIA COOKIES

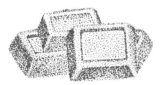

Add ¼ cup unsweetened cocoa powder to the batter after you've beaten in the sugar, and use 9 instead of 8 ounces of bittersweet chocolate, chunked. Omit the candied peel and use instead ½ cup chopped crystallized ginger. Use 1 generous cup of coarsely chopped macadamia nuts, not hazelnuts. Continue with the recipe as directed and bake the cookies for 10 to 12 minutes for chewy cookies, and for 13 to 15 minutes for crisp ones. These are intense.

LEMON DROPS

ABOUT 45 COOKIES

2 sticks (1 cup) unsalted butter, softened
½ cup confectioners' sugar
1 egg yolk
2 tablespoons fresh lemon juice
Grated zest of 1 lemon
2¼ cups all-purpose flour
Granulated sugar
Lemon Glaze (page 116) combined with 1 teaspoon grated lemon zest

These are buttery, lemony bites that almost melt in your mouth. A nice addition to any cookie basket for their fresh, tart flavor and pretty glazed tops.

Preheat the oven to 350° F. Line cookie sheets with parchment paper or butter them.

In a large bowl, cream the butter and confectioners' sugar with an electric mixer, add the egg yolk, lemon juice, and lemon zest and beat until smooth. Add the flour and beat until well combined.

Form the dough into 1-inch balls and place them about 2 inches apart on the prepared sheets. Flatten each ball with the bottom of a glass dipped into granulated sugar to keep it from sticking to the dough. Bake the cookies in the middle of the oven for about 13 minutes, or until barely golden. Transfer to wire racks. As soon as they are cool enough to handle, dip the top of each cookie in lemon glaze and allow to cool completely. Store in airtight containers for up to 1 week or in the freezer for up to 2 months.

SPLIT SECONDS

ABOUT 72 COOKIES

·

2 cups all-purpose flour
½ teaspoon baking powder
¼ teaspoon cinnamon
1½ sticks (¾ cup) unsalted butter,
    softened
⅔ cup granulated sugar
1 large egg
2 teaspoons vanilla extract
⅓ cup pecans or walnuts, finely
    chopped
⅓ cup raspberry or other jam

These came from our friend Mary Garrity's grandmother. We have since found out that these old-fashioned cookies are also called jelly splits. Mary's grandmother probably called them split seconds because they can be prepared and baked so quickly. The dough is formed into 4 logs, which are sliced after baking. They taste rich and look elegant, and your friends will think you spent a lot of time making them.

Preheat the oven to 350° F. Line a large cookie sheet with parchment paper or butter it.

On a piece of wax paper, combine the flour, baking powder, and cinnamon. In a large bowl, cream butter with an electric mixer, add the sugar, and continue beating until light and fluffy. Add the egg and vanilla and beat until smooth. Beat in the flour mixture until the dough is well mixed.

Turn the dough out onto a piece of wax paper and divide it into quarters. (The dough will be soft and very pliant. Once you place it on your cookie sheet, you'll be able to stretch it out, but you won't be able to pick it up and move it.)

Pick up a piece of dough and form it into a thick sausage shape with your hands. Place it on the cookie sheet about 2 inches from one of the long edges. Use your fingers to stretch the dough into a narrow log about 13 inches long and about ¾ inch wide; the log need not be perfectly round. Sprinkle one-quarter of the chopped nuts on top of the log and gently press them into the surface of the dough. Using the edge of your pinky finger, make a trough about ¼ inch deep down the length of the log. Fill the trough with jam. Repeat with the 3 remaining pieces of dough, leaving at least 3 inches between each log (they will spread during baking).

Bake in the middle of the oven for 13 to 18 minutes,

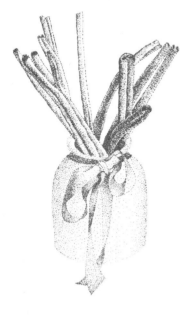

or until the logs start to color. With the logs still on the pan, cut each one diagonally into 18 slices while still warm. Slide the parchment paper off the pan onto a rack with the sliced logs still intact and allow to cool completely. Store in airtight containers for up to 1 week or in the freezer for up to 2 months.

Cinnamon Orange Coconut Cookies

60 COOKIES

∙

2½ cups all-purpose flour
2 teaspoons baking powder
¼ teaspoon salt
1½ teaspoons cinnamon
¼ cup vegetable shortening
½ stick (¼ cup) unsalted butter,
    softened
1 cup granulated sugar
2 large eggs
1 teaspoon orange extract
1½ cups flaked coconut
Cinnamon Sugar (page 120)
Chocolate Dipping Glaze
    (page 118), optional

As these cookies bake, the mingled scents of cinnamon, orange, and coconut remind us of warm tropical breezes.

Preheat oven to 375° F. Line cookie sheets with parchment paper or butter them.

On a piece of wax paper, combine flour, baking powder, salt, and cinnamon, and set aside. In a large bowl, cream the shortening and butter with an electric mixer, add the sugar and beat until light and fluffy. Add the eggs and orange extract and beat until well mixed. Add the flour mixture and beat until smooth. Stir in the coconut.

Divide the dough into quarters and cut each quarter into 15 pieces. Shape the pieces into 1-inch balls, roll them in the cinnamon sugar, and place them about 2 inches apart on the prepared cookie sheets. Flatten the balls of dough, using the bottom of a glass or the top of a wide jar. Bake in the middle of the oven for 8 to 10 minutes, or until the cookies are puffed. The cookies will be pale and soft to the touch when you remove them from the oven, but they'll firm up as they cool, so don't overbake. Transfer the cookies to racks to cool. For a decorator touch, dip one end of each cookie in chocolate dipping glaze. Store in an airtight container for up to 1 week or freeze for up to 2 months.

KOURABIEDES

64 COOKIES

.

4 sticks (2 cups) unsalted butter, softened

¾ cup confectioners' sugar, sifted

1 egg yolk

2 to 3 tablespoons Cognac or brandy

4½ cups sifted all-purpose flour

64 whole cloves

Sifted confectioners' sugar for dusting

Scented with brandy and whole cloves, these delicate Greek holiday cookies should be served within three or four days of baking.

In a large bowl, cream the butter very well, using an electric mixer. Gradually add the sugar and beat until the mixture is light and very smooth. Beat in the egg yolk and Cognac and continue beating until well mixed. Add the flour a little at a time, beating well after each addition, until the dough is smooth. With lightly floured hands, transfer the dough to a sheet of wax paper, form it into a ball, and wrap it in the wax paper. Chill the dough until firm but not hard, about 1 hour.

Preheat the oven to 350° F. Divide the dough into quarters and cut each quarter into 16 pieces. Roll each piece into a ball, arrange them on ungreased cookie sheets about 1½ inches apart, and stick a whole clove into the top of each cookie. (At this point, the cookies can be frozen for later baking, as discussed on page 27.) Bake the cookies in the middle of the oven for 10 to 13 minutes, or until barely colored at the edges. The cookies are very fragile just after baking; let them cool on the sheets for 3 or 4 minutes, then carefully transfer them to racks set over wax paper or newspaper. While they are still warm, dust the cookies generously with sifted confectioners' sugar. Store in airtight containers for up to 4 days.

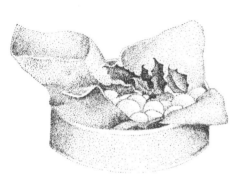

COCONUT CHOCOLATE CHIP TEA CAKES

48 COOKIES

∎

2 sticks (1 cup) unsalted butter,
   softened
½ cup sifted confectioners' sugar
1 teaspoon vanilla extract
2¼ cups sifted all-purpose flour
¼ teaspoon salt
1 cup shredded coconut
1 cup semisweet chocolate chips
48 pecan or walnut halves
Sifted confectioners' sugar for
   dusting

Barbara's Aunt Joyce contributed this recipe, in which the chocolate chip cookie is taken to new heights. The chips are barely visible after the cookies are baked, and their presence is further obscured by a dusting of confectioners' sugar. How pleasurable, then, to realize after your first bite that there's a chocolate surprise waiting just beneath the surface. Oh, they're luscious!

Preheat the oven to 350° F.

In a mixing bowl, cream the butter until light with an electric mixer, add the confectioners' sugar, and beat until the mixture is light and fluffy. Beat in the vanilla. Beat in the flour and salt, then add the coconut and beat until the dough is well mixed. Knead in the chocolate chips by hand.

Divide the dough into quarters and cut each quarter into 12 pieces. Roll the pieces into balls and place 1 inch apart on ungreased cookie sheets, then press a pecan half into the center of each cookie. (At this point, the cookies may be frozen for later baking; see page 27.)

Bake the cookies in the middle of the oven for 12 to 15 minutes, or until the edges begin to turn golden. Transfer to racks to cool and, while they are still warm, dust cookies very lightly with sifted confectioners' sugar. Store in airtight containers for up to 1 week.

ANGEL FINGERS

24 COOKIES

•

1 stick (½ cup) unsalted butter,
   softened
3 tablespoons confectioners' sugar
1 teaspoon vanilla extract
1 cup sifted cake flour
½ cup ground pistachios or pecans
All-purpose flour
Vanilla Confectioners' Sugar
   (page 119), for dusting

From the files of Lepha K. Gilbert, these adorably named cookies are short, buttery, and not too sweet. Although the dough is shaped into little fingers, as they bake the cookies flatten out into small ovals. We've made them with pecans and pistachios, and each version has its advocates. The pistachio cookies are faintly salty, the ones with pecans sumptuous.

Preheat the oven to 350° F.

In a mixing bowl, cream the butter with an electric mixer. Add the confectioners' sugar and beat until well mixed. Beat in the vanilla, then add the cake flour and ground nuts and mix well. Cover the dough with wax paper and refrigerate for 10 or 15 minutes, or until it firms up.

Divide the dough in half and cut each half into 12 pieces. Place some all-purpose flour on a sheet of wax paper and use it to dust your hands lightly before shaping each cookie. Form the dough into little rolls, about 1½ inches long and ½ inch in diameter, and place the cookies on ungreased baking sheets about 1½ inches apart. Bake in the middle of the oven for about 13 minutes, or until pale golden around the edges.

Transfer the angel fingers to racks set over wax paper or newspaper and dust them with vanilla confectioners' sugar while still warm. Cool the cookies completely and store in airtight containers for up to 1 week.

COOKIE SAMPLER

•

BARBARA'S BROWNIES
page 51

GINGER PECAN SLICES
page 75

ANGEL FINGERS
page 44

SWEDISH BUTTER COOKIES

44 OR 48 COOKIES

■

1¾ cups sifted all-purpose flour
½ teaspoon baking powder
½ cup ground unblanched
    almonds
¼ teaspoon salt
1½ sticks (¾ cup) unsalted butter,
    softened
½ cup plus 2 tablespoons packed
    dark brown sugar
1 large egg, separated
1 teaspoon vanilla extract
1 tablespoon water
1⅓ cups sliced unblanched
    almonds
Sparkling jelly or preserves

Wonderfully rich and buttery, these thumbprint cookies freeze very well. Some recipes call for making the thumbprint indentations before the cookies go into the oven, but we've found that those indentations fill in during the early stages of baking, and the most reliable method is the one we use: pressing the back of a measuring half-teaspoon into the top of each cookie when the pan is rotated halfway through baking.

Preheat the oven to 350° F. Line cookie sheets with parchment paper or butter them.

Combine the flour, baking powder, ground almonds, and salt on a sheet of wax paper and set aside. In a mixing bowl with an electric mixer, cream the butter, add the brown sugar, and continue beating until light. Beat in the egg yolk and vanilla. Add the dry ingredients to the creamed mixture and beat until the dough is well blended, using your hands in the final mixing.

In a bowl, beat the egg white and water with a fork or small whisk until frothy. Spread the sliced almonds on a sheet of wax paper. Divide the dough into quarters and cut each quarter into 11 or 12 pieces. Form the dough into balls and dip them into the egg white and then into the almonds. Place the cookies about 1½ inches apart on the prepared sheets and bake in the middle of the oven for 8 minutes. Remove from the oven and press the back of a measuring half-teaspoon or a small melon baller into the top of each cookie to form an indentation. Return the cookies to the oven and bake for 8 minutes longer, or until a rich golden brown. Transfer the cookies to racks to cool completely.

Fill as many cookies as you plan to serve that day with about ¼ teaspoon each of jelly or preserves. Store the unfilled cookies for up to 5 days in an airtight container and for up to 2 months in the freezer.

APRICOT-COCONUT CONFECTIONS

32 TO 36 CONFECTIONS

·

8 ounces dried apricots, ground
    medium-fine (about 1½ cups)
2 cups shredded coconut
⅔ cup sweetened condensed milk
Confectioners' sugar
4 ounces semisweet chocolate
    chips, melted (optional)

Barbara's mother, Adrianne, always made these at Christmastime. These are great to make with kids—the best part is rolling the pleasantly sticky mixture into balls.

Use soft, tender dried apricots for these easy-to-make, delicious morsels. Decorated with arabesques of melted chocolate and nestled in petit four cases, the confections are a pretty addition to a holiday cookie basket.

Line a baking sheet or platter with wax paper. If desired, spread out 32 to 36 foil-backed petit four cases on the wax paper.

Place the apricots and coconut in a mixing bowl, and blend by hand, breaking up the coconut and combining it well with the apricots. Add the condensed milk and stir with a spoon or by hand until the mixture is well combined.

Roll the mixture between your palms into balls about 1¼ inches in diameter and place them on wax paper.

Sift confectioners' sugar into a bowl and roll the balls in the sugar, tapping off the excess. Place the balls on the prepared baking sheet, putting them into the petit four cases if you're using them, and refrigerate until firm.

To decorate the confections, fill a small pastry bag fitted with the smallest writing tip with the hot melted chocolate. Pipe thin spirals and arabesques of chocolate over the tops of the confections and refrigerate again for at least 3 to 4 hours before serving. Store in airtight containers, separated by sheets of wax paper, for 3 to 4 days in the refrigerator or freeze for up to 1 month.

BAR COOKIES

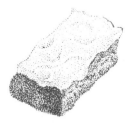

Bar cookies are a clever way of baking cakes, pies, and tarts so that they can be served attractively in manageable portions. Because the cookies are so concentrated in flavor and intensely rich, we recommend cutting them into very small pieces. For gifts, the squares look very appealing nestled in foil petit four cases.

The easiest way to cut bar cookies is with the blade of a metal pastry scraper. The blade makes a single clean cut right through frosting or glaze, filling, and crust. When the blade touches the bottom of the pan, rock it back and forth gently to loosen the crust from the pan.

Several of the cookies in this chapter freeze well, which makes them good candidates for advance preparation when you have an hour or two to spare.

LEMON-FROSTED WALNUT BARS

48 TO 54 PIECES

CRUST
2 cups all-purpose flour
½ cup packed light brown sugar
1 teaspoon cinnamon
2 sticks (1 cup) unsalted butter,
   cut into 16 pieces

FILLING
1½ cups packed light brown sugar
2 tablespoons all-purpose flour
½ teaspoon cinnamon
¼ teaspoon baking powder
¼ teaspoon salt
2 large eggs
1 teaspoon vanilla extract
1½ cups walnuts, coarsely
   chopped

FROSTING
2 tablespoons unsalted butter,
   softened
1½ cups confectioners' sugar
1 tablespoon fresh lemon juice
2 tablespoons fresh orange juice
½ cup walnuts, toasted and finely
   chopped

A flaky pastry crust, made with a touch of cinnamon, is topped with a moist walnut-studded filling and frosted with a tart lemon glaze.

For the crust: Preheat the oven to 350° F. With a food processor or electric mixer, combine the flour, brown sugar, and cinnamon. Add the butter and process until the mixture forms a smooth dough. Turn out into a 9 × 13-inch pan and, using your fingers or the palm of your hand, press the dough evenly over the bottom of the pan. Bake in the middle of the oven for 15 minutes, or until the crust just begins to turn tan.

While the crust is baking, prepare the filling: With an electric mixer, combine the brown sugar, flour, cinnamon, baking powder, and salt. Beat in the eggs, one at a time, beat in the vanilla, and stir in the walnuts. As soon as you have removed the crust from the oven, pour the filling mixture over the baked crust and spread it evenly over the crust. Return the pan to the oven and bake for 20 minutes more, or until the top of the filling has tanned evenly and is just firm to the touch. Place the pan on a wire rack and cool the cake completely before frosting.

For the frosting: In a small bowl, cream the butter. Beat in ½ cup of the confectioners' sugar, whisking until smooth, then stir in the lemon juice and orange juice. Add the remaining confectioners' sugar, ½ cup at a time, beating until smooth after each addition. If the mixture seems too thick to spread easily, stir in a little more lemon juice. Spread the frosting evenly over the cooled cake and sprinkle with the toasted walnuts. Cut into 48 to 54 pieces, using a pastry scraper with a metal blade, if possible. Store in an airtight container at room temperature for up to 2 days, in the refrigerator for up to 4 days, or in the freezer for up to 2 months.

BARBARA'S BROWNIES

■

*1 tablespoon unsweetened cocoa
     powder*
1½ cups all-purpose flour
½ teaspoon baking soda
¼ teaspoon salt
6 ounces unsweetened chocolate
*1½ sticks (¾ cup) unsalted butter,
     softened*
*1 tablespoon unsweetened
     cappuccino mix or instant
     coffee powder*
3 large eggs
1¼ cups granulated sugar
1 cup packed light brown sugar
1 tablespoon vanilla extract
*2 cups nuts, coarsely chopped
     (⅔ cup each unblanched
     whole almonds, walnuts,
     pecans)*
*6 ounces best quality bittersweet
     or semisweet chocolate,
     coarsely chopped with a knife*

It's no coincidence that Barbara's grandmother's maiden name was Fudge. Barbara's mom's brownies were the inspiration for this recipe, which was the hands-down winner in our taste test. These moist, superrich, fudgy morsels have too much of everything in them: There's too much chocolate, too much vanilla, and too many nuts, and that's just the way we like them.

Preheat the oven to 325° F. Butter the bottom and sides of a 9 × 13-inch pan and line the bottom with wax paper. Butter the paper and dust the pan with the cocoa powder.

On a piece of wax paper, combine the flour, baking soda, and salt. In the top of a double boiler over barely simmering water, melt the unsweetened chocolate, butter, and cappuccino mix. Set aside.

In a large mixing bowl, using an electric mixer, beat the eggs, sugars, and vanilla at high speed for 15 minutes. At low speed beat in the cooled chocolate mixture. Gradually add the flour mixture, and stir in the nuts and chopped bittersweet chocolate.

Spread the mixture evenly in the prepared pan and bake in the middle of the oven for 33 minutes. Transfer the pan to a wire rack and let the cake cool in the pan completely. When cool, run a sharp knife around the edge of the pan, and invert the cake onto a piece of wax paper. Peel off the wax paper from the bottom of the cake, and carefully turn the cake right-side up. Using a metal-bladed pastry scraper, cut the cake into small pieces. Store, tightly covered, in the refrigerator for up to 1 week.

BLUE RIBBON PECAN FUDGIES

48 TO 60 PIECES

.

CRUST

¼ cup pecans or walnuts, finely
    chopped
⅔ cup confectioners' sugar
2 cups all-purpose flour
2 sticks (1 cup) unsalted butter,
    cut into 8 pieces

FILLING

3 ounces unsweetened chocolate
1 stick (½ cup) unsalted butter
¾ cup packed dark brown sugar
¾ cup dark corn syrup
1½ teaspoons vanilla extract
1 tablespoon brandy, cognac, or
    dark rum
3 cups pecan halves or walnuts,
    coarsely chopped

Are they brownies? Are they pecan pie? Are they fudge? We've awarded ourselves the blue ribbon for these elegant and addictive little squares. Cut them *very* small; they look adorable nestled in foil candy or petit four cups.

Prepare the crust: Place the chopped nuts, confectioners' sugar, and flour in the bowl of a food processor fitted with the steel blade and pulse 2 or 3 times to mix. Arrange the butter pieces over the flour mixture and process just until a dough forms, about 30 seconds; the mixture should not form a ball around the shaft of the processor. Turn the dough out into a 9 × 13-inch baking pan and, using your fingers or the palm of your hand, press evenly over the bottom of the pan. Set aside.

Preheat the oven to 350° F.

Prepare the filling: In a small, heavy saucepan, melt the chocolate and butter over moderately low heat. Transfer the mixture to a bowl, add the brown sugar, corn syrup, vanilla, and brandy, and beat until smooth with a wooden spoon. Stir in the nuts and reserve.

Bake the crust in the middle of the oven for about 20 minutes, or until it is a light golden color. Remove the crust from the oven and immediately spread the filling evenly over the hot crust with a spatula. (Once the crust has begun to cool, it will shrink from the sides of the pan, leaving space for the filling to drip down to the bottom of the pan, making it difficult later on to cut squares and dislodge them from the pan.) The filling will be quite stiff; spread it carefully, taking care not to crush the tender crust.

Bake in the middle of the oven for 20 to 25 minutes, or until the filling is bubbly all over. Remove from the oven and, when the bubbling stops, run a sharp paring knife around the edge of the pan to separate the filling from the pan as it cools. If you wait until the filling cools, you will have

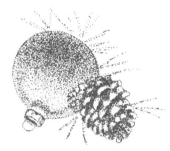

trouble removing the squares from the pan. Place the pan on a rack and let the pastry and filling cool completely before cutting into 1- to 1½-inch squares. (A pastry scraper with a metal blade will make this task easier.) Store the fudgies in an airtight container at room temperature for up to 2 days, in the refrigerator for up to 1 week, or in the freezer for up to 2 months.

JACKIE'S LEMON COCONUT PECAN BARS

36 SQUARES

CRUST
1 cup all-purpose flour
⅛ teaspoon salt
2 teaspoons granulated sugar
2 sticks (1 cup) unsalted butter,
    cut into 8 pieces

FILLING
2 large eggs
1 cup packed dark brown sugar
1 cup flaked coconut
½ cup chopped pecans
1 tablespoon fresh lemon juice
Grated zest of ½ lemon

GLAZE
⅔ cup sifted confectioners' sugar
1½ to 2 tablespoons fresh lemon
    juice
Grated zest of ½ lemon

Jackie Montgomery learned to make these fabulous lemon squares when she was about ten years old, and she's been serving them to eager takers for many years at her Christmas Eve party.

Preheat the oven to 350° F.

To make the crust, combine the flour, salt, and granulated sugar in a food processor fitted with the steel blade. Pulse 3 or 4 times to mix, then distribute the butter pieces over the mixture. Pulse the machine for 5 or 6 long bursts, or until the mixture resembles cornmeal. Press the dough evenly into a 9-inch-square baking pan and bake in the middle of the oven for 15 minutes, or until very lightly golden.

To make the filling, in a mixing bowl beat the eggs, add the brown sugar, coconut, pecans, lemon juice, and lemon zest, and beat again until well mixed. Pour the filling over the baked crust and bake for 30 minutes.

Meanwhile, prepare the glaze: In a bowl combine the confectioners' sugar with enough lemon juice to make a spreadable consistency, add the lemon zest, and mix well. When the pan is out of the oven, spread the glaze evenly on top. Place the pan on a rack and cool before cutting into 1½-inch squares. Store in the refrigerator for up to 1 week.

RASPBERRY OR APRICOT BARS WITH A LATTICE CRUST

24 BARS

·

BOTTOM CRUST
½ cup confectioners' sugar
1½ cups all-purpose flour
1½ sticks (¾ cup) unsalted butter,
    cut into 12 pieces

LATTICE CRUST
½ cup confectioners' sugar
1¾ cups all-purpose flour
1½ sticks (¾ cup) unsalted butter,
    cut into 12 pieces

FILLING
1⅔ cups raspberry or apricot
    preserves

2 tablespoons milk or half-and-
    half cream for brushing the
    lattice crust

Barbara used to make these bars for a local market, and they were her most popular cookie. In addition to tasting great, they look pretty and festive with the brightly colored jam filling showing between the golden strips of lattice crust.

We make these bars in a 7 × 11-inch pan because the lattice dough is somewhat fragile and therefore more manageable in short lengths. Use the best quality preserves that you can find; you'll agree they were well worth the price when you taste the results.

Preheat the oven to 350° F.

For the bottom crust: In the bowl of a food processor fitted with the steel blade, pulse the sugar and flour just to combine. Distribute the pieces of butter evenly on top of the flour mixture, pulse 3 or 4 times to mix, then process until a smooth dough is formed. Transfer the dough to a 7 × 11-inch baking pan, pat it evenly into the bottom of the pan, and bake in the middle of the oven for 20 minutes, or until the crust just starts to turn light golden.

While the bottom crust is baking, prepare the dough for the lattice crust, using the same procedure as that used for the bottom crust. Turn the dough out onto a lightly floured work surface or sheet of wax paper and roll it out into a 15 × 7-inch rectangle. With a sharp knife, cut the dough lengthwise into 7 strips. You'll use 4 of these as is for the long lattice strips. Cut the remaining 3 strips in half crosswise to use for the short lattice strips (you'll need only 5 short strips, so the sixth strip will be for patching, if necessary).

When the bottom crust has baked for 20 minutes, remove it from the oven, and carefully spread the preserves evenly on top of the crust, leaving a border of crust about ¼ inch around the edge. (If the filling is spread right to the edge of the crust, it will ooze down between the crust and the sides of the pan as it bakes and will stick to the pan, making it difficult to dislodge the bars.)

Using a long, thin-bladed metal spatula, carefully place the lattice strips over the jam. Start with the long strips. Place 1 strip lengthwise next to one long edge of the pan. Place a second strip along the opposite long edge of the pan, place the third and fourth strips between the first two, leaving equal space between each of the strips. Trim the strips to fit the length of the pan. Brush the strips with milk or half-and-half. Next, position the short strips across and on top of the long strips. You'll be using 5 short strips. Place 1 strip next to one short edge of the pan, place the second strip along the opposite short edge, place the third strip in the center between the first two, and place the fourth and fifth strips centered in the spaces between the center and end strips. Trim the excess dough and brush the top of the strips with milk.

Bake in the middle of the oven for 20 minutes more, or until the crust is golden. Let the bars cool in the pan before cutting lengthwise into 4 strips and crosswise into 6 strips, for a total of 24 pieces. If some of the filling has oozed down between the crust and the edge of the pan, run a sharp knife around the edge of the pan while the bars are still hot to make it easier to remove them from the pan once they have cooled.

Store the bars in the refrigerator for up to 1 week or freeze them for up to 2 months.

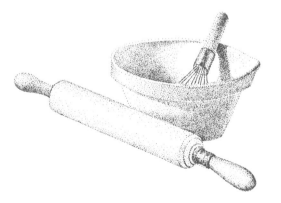

RASPBERRY SQUARES

48 SQUARES

▪

CRUST

*1½ sticks (¾ cup) unsalted butter,
    softened*
⅓ cup granulated sugar
2 egg yolks
1½ cups sifted all-purpose flour

TOPPING

*1 cup good-quality seedless
    raspberry jam, homemade
    currant preserves, or other
    jam or preserves*
2 egg whites
½ cup granulated sugar
1 cup finely chopped nuts

A tender, buttery crust is baked until firm, then spread with jam or preserves, topped with a Swiss meringue, and baked again. We tested three different recipes for this Eastern European Christmas cookie before Charlotte Katelvero sent us this simple and scrumptiously delicious version. The cookies deserve the very best jam or preserves you can get, preferably not too sweet, because there's so much sugar already in the crust and meringue.

Preheat the oven to 350° F. Butter a 9 × 13-inch baking pan.

To make the crust, in a mixing bowl cream the butter with an electric mixer, add the sugar, and continue beating until light and fluffy. Beat in the egg yolks, then add the flour and beat until very well mixed. Pat the dough evenly into the prepared pan, building up a ½-inch rim around the sides of the pan. Bake in the middle of the oven for 15 minutes, or until the edges just begin to turn golden.

Remove the crust from the oven, but leave the heat on. Let the crust cool for 2 to 3 minutes, then spread with the jam. In a mixing bowl, beat the egg whites with an electric mixer until soft peaks begin to form, then gradually add the sugar and beat until stiff. Fold in the nuts and spread the meringue over the jam, working from the rim of the pan toward the center. Bake in the middle of the oven for about 20 minutes, or until the meringue is light tan; begin watching carefully after 15 minutes to make sure that the meringue doesn't burn. Place the pan on a rack and let cool. Cut the cake into 1¼-inch squares, using a pastry scraper with a metal blade, if you have one (a sharp knife will do perfectly well, if you don't). Store, tightly covered, in the refrigerator for up to 4 days.

SQUARES (NANAIMO BARS)

81 1-INCH SQUARES

•

CRUST

1 stick (½ cup) unsalted butter,
    cut into 8 pieces
¼ cup granulated sugar
¼ cup unsweetened cocoa powder
1 teaspoon vanilla extract
1 large egg
¼ teaspoon salt
1½ cups graham cracker crumbs
¾ cup flaked coconut
⅓ cup pecans, chopped

FILLING

1 stick (½ cup) unsalted butter,
    softened
3 ounces cream cheese
2 tablespoons instant vanilla
    pudding powder
1 cup confectioners' sugar, sifted
2 tablespoons milk

GLAZE

4 ounces unsweetened chocolate
1 tablespoon unsalted butter

This recipe is a traditional and much anticipated holiday treat in the household of Barbara's Aunt Joyce. The squares are very sweet and absolutely delicious—as much a confection as they are a cookie.

Line the bottom of a 9-inch-square baking pan with a piece of wax or parchment paper cut long enough to extend up and over the two opposite sides of the pan, to make it easier to remove the squares from the pan.

For the crust: In a heavy saucepan, combine the butter, granulated sugar, cocoa powder, vanilla, egg, and salt. Stir with a wooden spoon until the mixture is smooth (except for the butter, which will still be in chunks). Cook over low heat, stirring constantly, until the butter is melted and the mixture has thickened slightly, 3 to 5 minutes. Remove the pan from the heat and stir in the graham cracker crumbs, coconut, and pecans. Pour the mixture into the prepared pan and spread it evenly over the bottom.

For the filling: In a large bowl, cream the butter, cream cheese, and pudding powder with an electric mixer. Add the confectioners' sugar and milk and beat until smooth. Spread the mixture evenly over the crust. Cover with wax paper and refrigerate for 30 minutes, or until the filling is firm.

For the glaze: Melt the chocolate and butter in the top of a double boiler over simmering water. Spread the glaze evenly on top of the filling, cover again, and refrigerate until firm.

Cut into 1-inch squares, preferably with a metal-bladed pastry scraper, and refrigerate again for about 30 minutes before removing squares from pan. Store in the refrigerator for 1 week or in the freezer for up to 1 month.

DATE-NUT BARS

1 cup all-purpose flour
1 teaspoon baking powder
⅛ teaspoon salt
1 pound pitted dates
1 cup chopped walnuts (preferably
    English walnuts)
3 large eggs, separated
1 cup granulated sugar
2 to 3 cups sifted confectioners'
    sugar

Cut into small squares and tossed in confectioners' sugar, these old-fashioned chewy cookies taste almost like candy. The original recipe called for cutting the dates into quarters, a tedious process, so we've opted for chopping them in a food processor. Don't be tempted to use packaged chopped dates—they're far too sweet and scarcely taste like real fruit.

Preheat the oven to 350° F. Generously butter a 9 × 13-inch baking pan.

Sift the flour, baking powder, and salt onto a sheet of wax paper. To chop the dates, place one-third or one-quarter of them in a food processor fitted with the steel blade, sprinkle the fruit with 2 tablespoons of the flour mixture, and pulse the machine until the dates are very coarsely chopped. Transfer the chopped dates to another piece of wax paper and chop the remaining dates in the same way. Add the nuts to the dates and combine.

In a mixing bowl with an electric mixer, beat the egg whites until stiff but not dry, and reserve. In another mixing bowl, beat the egg yolks until well mixed, add the granulated sugar gradually, and continue beating until the mixture is lemon-colored and very thick. Add the dates and nuts and combine with the egg yolk mixture by hand or, if you are using a heavy-duty mixer, with the flat beater. Add the flour mixture and combine well with the fruit mixture; at this point it may be easiest to work with your hands because even a heavy-duty mixer will be strained. Add the egg whites and fold them in with your hand, evenly moistening the flour-and-egg-yolk-coated fruit and nuts. By now, the mixture should resemble a sticky, jam-like mass rather than a dough.

Spread the mixture evenly in the prepared pan and bake in the middle of the oven for 18 to 24 minutes, or until the top is golden brown and still soft to the touch.

COOKIE SAMPLER

•

DATE-NUT BARS
page 58

CRANBERRY COOKIES
page 22

KOURABIEDES
page 42

Cool in the pan for about 5 minutes, then invert on a rack and cool. Cut into 80 squares (a metal-bladed pastry scraper will make this task easier). Roll the squares in the confectioners' sugar, coating them completely. Shake off the excess sugar and store in layers that are separated by wax paper in an airtight container, for up to 3 weeks.

ICEBOX COOKIES

Icebox cookies are rich in butter, and because many of them are made with either confectioners' sugar or cake flour (both of which contain cornstarch), they are often quite silky in texture.

By definition, icebox cookies must be refrigerated before they're sliced and baked, and the dough is even easier to slice when it's frozen. If you're instantly gratified by cutting a few slices off a log of butter-scotch cookies and baking them right from the freezer, this chapter is for you. Should there be any leftovers, the baked cookies freeze well, too.

POPPY SEED COOKIES

60 TO 65 COOKIES

·

2 sticks (1 cup) unsalted butter,
 softened
1 cup sifted confectioners' sugar
1 teaspoon vanilla extract
¼ cup poppy seeds
1½ teaspoons grated lemon zest
2 cups all-purpose flour
¼ teaspoon salt

Judy says her grandmother made the best poppy seed cookies she ever tasted. Although we've been unable to duplicate that recipe, these crisp and meltingly delicious icebox cookies run a close second.

Cream the butter in a large mixing bowl, using an electric mixer. Add the sugar and beat until light and fluffy. Beat in the vanilla, then add the poppy seeds, lemon zest, flour, and salt and stir until the dough is very well mixed. Turn the dough out on a work surface and form into 2 or 3 rough logs, about 1½ to 1¾ inches in diameter. Wrap the logs in wax paper and refrigerate for 30 minutes, or until firm enough to shape into smooth, even rolls. Rewrap the rolls in wax paper and refrigerate for another hour or two, or put into heavy plastic bags and freeze.

Preheat the oven to 375° F. Remove the rolls from the refrigerator one at a time, place on a cutting board, and cut into slices just under ¼ inch thick. Arrange the slices on ungreased cookie sheets about 1 inch apart and bake in the middle of the oven for 8 to 10 minutes, or just until the edges turn golden. Transfer the cookies to racks to cool. Store at room temperature for 1 week in an airtight container and up to 2 months in the freezer.

COOKIE SAMPLER
·

PEPPARKAKOR COOKIES
page 102

**COCONUT
CHOCOLATE CHIP
TEA CAKES**
page 43

POPPY SEED COOKIES
page 64

BUTTERSCOTCH COOKIES

ABOUT 70 COOKIES

∎

2½ cups cake flour
1 teaspoon baking powder
½ teaspoon salt
½ cup chopped nuts
1¾ sticks (⅞ cup) unsalted butter
1 cup packed light brown sugar
1 large egg
1 teaspoon vanilla extract

Melted butter, brown sugar, and chopped nuts produce a seductive butterscotch flavor in this old-time recipe from Vermont.

Combine the flour, baking powder, salt, and nuts in a bowl and set aside. In a small, heavy saucepan over moderately low heat, melt the butter and simmer it slowly until it is a deep golden yellow and the sediment at the bottom has browned very slightly. Shake the pan occasionally to prevent the sediment from burning. Pour the melted butter into a measuring cup (strain it through a small cheesecloth-lined sieve if the sediment has burned), then pour ¾ cup of it into a heatproof mixing bowl. Add the brown sugar and beat until well mixed. Allow the mixture to stand until warm, but not hot, and add the egg, beating vigorously until the mixture is the consistency of mayonnaise. Beat in the vanilla. Add the flour mixture in thirds and beat until well combined.

Turn the dough out on a work surface and form into 2 logs 1½ inches in diameter. Wrap the logs in wax paper and refrigerate for about 30 minutes, then shape them into smooth, even rolls, rewrap in wax paper and then in foil, and freeze for 2 hours.

Preheat the oven to 375° F. Remove the rolls from the refrigerator one at a time, place on a cutting board, and with a sharp knife cut into slices just under ¼ inch thick. Arrange the cookies 1½ inches apart on ungreased cookie sheets. Bake for 9 to 11 minutes in the middle of the oven, or just until the edges of the cookies are golden. Transfer to racks to cool. Store in an airtight container for 1 week, or freeze for up to 2 months.

DOUBLE CHOCOLATE WAFERS

ABOUT 140 SMALL COOKIES

.

6 ounces bittersweet or semisweet
  chocolate
2¼ cups all-purpose flour
½ teaspoon baking powder
⅛ teaspoon salt
2 sticks (1 cup) unsalted butter,
  softened
⅔ cup superfine granulated sugar
1 large egg
1½ teaspoons vanilla extract
1 cup finely chopped nuts

These were originally intended as spritz cookies. We whipped up the dough at the end of a very long day, filled the cookie press, and inserted a disk. Spritz, spritz, spritz—but all that came out were anemic strands of dough because, you see, the chopped chocolate and nuts were clogging the holes in the disk. "Tomorrow is another day," one of us muttered (the other screamed), and we scraped the dough out of the press, hastily slapped it into a roll, and stored it in the refrigerator overnight. The rest is history.

For triple chocolate wafers, dip the cooled cookies into melted bittersweet chocolate and then into more chopped nuts (see Mochaccinos, page 82).

In the top of a double boiler, melt 2 ounces of the chocolate over hot water. Remove from heat and set aside. In a food processor fitted with the steel blade, finely chop the remaining 4 ounces of chocolate and set aside.

Combine the flour, baking powder, and salt on a sheet of wax paper and set aside. In a large mixing bowl, use an electric mixer to cream the butter until light. Add the sugar and beat until the mixture is fluffy. Beat in the egg and vanilla. Add the cooled melted chocolate and beat until very well mixed. Add the flour mixture and beat until the dough is smooth. Beat in the chopped chocolate and nuts.

Divide the dough into thirds or quarters, form each piece into a rough rectangular log, and wrap in wax paper. Refrigerate the logs for about 30 minutes, then reshape them into smooth rectangles about ¾ inch thick and 1½ to 2 inches wide. (If you prefer, you can form the dough into round logs about 1½ inches in diameter.) Rewrap in wax paper and refrigerate the dough for 2 hours, or until very firm, or place the wrapped dough in freezer bags and store in the freezer for up to 2 months.

Preheat the oven to 375° F. Cut each log into thin slices, between ⅛ and ¼ inch thick, and arrange the cookies on an ungreased cookie sheet about ¾ inch apart. Bake in the middle of the oven for about 8 minutes, or until the cookies are a dark mocha color; they should not brown. Transfer them to racks to cool. Store in airtight containers for 10 days or in the freezer for up to 2 months.

ROLLED DOUBLE CHOCOLATE COOKIES

This dough is easy to roll out and looks charming cut into shapes and decorated—before baking with silver dragées or after baking with white icing or melted chocolate. Divide the finished dough into quarters and flatten into disks. Wrap in wax paper and refrigerate for about 30 minutes, or until firm enough to roll out, but not rock-hard. Roll out the dough between unfloured sheets of wax paper to a generous ⅛ inch thickness. Remove the top layer of paper and cut the dough into shapes. Decorate at this point if you wish, then slide the sheet of wax paper onto a baking sheet and refrigerate for about 10 minutes, or until the dough is firm enough not to tear when you prize the cut shapes away from the scraps with an icing spatula. Bake the cookies on ungreased cookie sheets as described above. Makes 60 to 70 medium-sized cookies.

COOKIE SAMPLER
·

**BLUE RIBBON
PECAN FUDGIES**
page 52

**CHOCOLATE PECAN
BROWNIE KISSES**
page 13

**DOUBLE CHOCOLATE
WAFERS**
page 66

BROWNED BUTTER ICEBOX COOKIES

ABOUT 70 COOKIES

2 sticks (1 cup) unsalted butter
2 cups all-purpose flour
2½ tablespoons cornstarch
1 teaspoon baking powder
¼ teaspoon salt
⅔ cup granulated sugar
1 large egg
1 teaspoon vanilla extract

COOKIE SAMPLER

Browned butter imparts an intense, nutty flavor. Because they are so rich, we make these cookies quite small— about 1½ inches in diameter. The master recipe and both variations are delicious, but we especially love the cappuccino cookies, which are made with unsweetened instant cappuccino mix. Read the label on the jar carefully; if the first ingredient is sugar, it's not what you want.

In a small, heavy saucepan, melt the butter over moderate heat and brown it, skimming the foam from the top as the butter simmers. Do not allow the butter to burn. Strain it through a fine sieve into a large mixing bowl and allow to cool.

Sift the flour, cornstarch, baking powder, and salt onto a piece of wax paper and set aside. Add the sugar to the cooled melted butter and beat until well mixed. Add the egg and vanilla and beat until the mixture is thick and the consistency of mayonnaise. Add the flour mixture in thirds, beating well after each addition, until the dough clears the sides of the bowl.

The dough will be quite soft. Divide it into 2 or 3 pieces, roll each piece into a rough log, and wrap the logs individually in wax paper. Refrigerate for about 30 minutes to firm up the dough, then form it into smooth rolls 1¼ to 1½ inches in diameter, using wax paper to even them up. Refrigerate the dough again for at least 3 hours or overnight, or freeze for about 2 hours, or until very firm. (If you plan to keep the dough frozen for longer than overnight, store it in freezer bags as well as wax paper.)

Preheat the oven to 375° F. Remove one roll at a time from the refrigerator and cut it into scant ¼-inch slices. Arrange the cookies 1 inch apart on ungreased cookie sheets and bake in the middle of the oven for 10 to 13 minutes, or until golden brown around the edges. Transfer to racks to cool. Store at room temperature in an airtight container for up to 1 week and in freezer bags for up to 2 months.

SPICED ICEBOX COOKIES

Sift 1½ teaspoons cinnamon and ¾ teaspoon each ginger, allspice, and freshly grated nutmeg with the flour mixture. If you prefer a slightly more intense flavor, add 1 to 2 teaspoons molasses with the egg.

CAPPUCCINO ICEBOX COOKIES

Mix ½ cup unsweetened instant cappuccino mix into the sugar before adding it to the melted butter. Add 2 teaspoons molasses with the egg and vanilla.

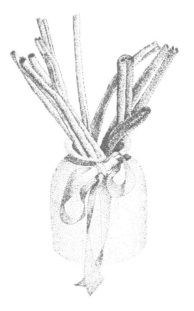

PINWHEELS

60 TO 70 PINWHEELS AND ABOUT 15 MARBLE COOKIES

·

ORANGE DOUGH

1½ cups all-purpose flour
½ teaspoon baking powder
¼ teaspoon salt
½ cup ground blanched almonds
1 stick (½ cup) unsalted butter,
  softened
½ cup granulated sugar
½ cup packed light brown sugar
1 large egg
1 teaspoon orange extract
1 tablespoon grated orange zest

CHOCOLATE DOUGH

1½ cups all-purpose flour
½ teaspoon baking powder
½ teaspoon cinnamon
¼ teaspoon salt
1 stick (½ cup) unsalted butter,
  softened
½ cup granulated sugar
½ cup packed dark brown sugar
1 large egg
1 teaspoon vanilla extract
3 ounces unsweetened chocolate,
  melted
3 ounces very finely chopped
  bittersweet or semisweet
  chocolate

Most pinwheel recipes call for making a single dough, dividing it in half, and adding chocolate to one of the pieces. The challenge we set for ourselves in developing this recipe was to come up with two different doughs, which nevertheless would complement each other in flavor and texture, and chocolate and orange seemed to be a natural combination. These doughs work together perfectly as pinwheels, and they look just as intriguing combined freely into logs and sliced into marble cookies. Each dough is delicious enough to be used as a single-flavor icebox cookie.

For the orange dough: On a sheet of wax paper, combine the flour, baking powder, salt, and ground almonds, and set aside. In a large mixing bowl, cream the butter with an electric mixer, add the sugars, and continue beating until light. Add the egg, orange extract, and grated zest and beat well. Add the flour mixture and beat until the dough is smooth. Form into a ball, place on a sheet of wax paper larger than 9 × 13 inches, and reserve while you make the chocolate dough.

For the chocolate dough: Combine the flour, baking powder, cinnamon, and salt on a sheet of wax paper and set aside. In a large mixing bowl with an electric mixer, cream the butter, add the sugars, and beat until light. Add the egg and vanilla and beat well. Beat in the melted chocolate. Add the flour mixture and beat until the dough is well mixed. Stir in the finely chopped chocolate. Form the dough into a ball and place on a sheet of wax paper.

Place the sheet of wax paper with the orange dough in a 9 × 13-inch baking pan, paper side down. Using your hands, press the paper into the corners of the pan, then press the dough evenly over the bottom of the pan. Place the chocolate dough, still on its sheet of wax paper, on the counter and, with your hands, press it into an even rectangle slightly smaller than the baking pan. Invert the chocolate dough over the orange dough. You will now have 2 layers of dough sandwiched between 2 sheets of wax paper. Gently smooth the chocolate layer to cover the surface of the orange layer. Lift the dough out of the pan, using the bottom sheet of wax paper, and put the layers, orange side down, on the work surface, keeping both sheets of wax paper in place. Use your rolling pin to press the two layers of dough together and to flatten them to an even thickness of about ⅜ inch. The dough will probably spread unevenly, but never mind; you're going to trim it. Remove the top layer of wax paper and turn the dough so that a long side of the rectangle faces you. With a sharp knife, trim the edges to form a straight-sided rectangle and save the scraps for marble cookies (below).

Lift the edge of the bottom sheet of wax paper nearest you and begin to roll the dough into a smooth, compact cylinder about 3 inches in diameter, smoothing out the dough with the wax paper as you roll it. Trim the ends of the cylinder, saving the scraps. Wrap the cylinder of dough in wax paper and refrigerate for 45 minutes. Smooth out the cylinder again, rewrap it, and refrigerate the dough for 3 hours or overnight.

Preheat the oven to 375° F. Line cookie sheets with parchment paper or butter them.

With a sharp knife, cut the cylinder of dough into slices ⅛ to ¼ inch thick and arrange 1 inch apart on the prepared sheets. Bake in the middle of the oven for about 8 minutes, or until the cookies barely begin to color at the edges. Transfer to racks to cool. Store in airtight containers for up to 1 week or freeze for up to 2 months.

MARBLE COOKIES

Press the pinwheel scraps together and form into a log about 2 inches in diameter. Wrap in wax paper and refrigerate for 2 hours. Slice ⅛ to ¼ inch thick and bake as directed above.

ORANGE AND CHOCOLATE TWISTS

Instead of rolling the two layers of dough into a cylinder, cut into strips ½ inch wide and 4 inches long. Twist the dough strips into loose corkscrews and bake as directed above.

Neapolitans

DARK DOUGH

3 cups sifted all-purpose flour
¼ teaspoon salt
1 teaspoon baking soda
½ teaspoon cinnamon
½ teaspoon ground cloves
1 tablespoon unsweetened instant
    cappuccino powder or instant
    coffee powder
1 cup walnuts, pecans, or
    almonds, coarsely ground
6 ounces semisweet chocolate
    chips, chilled and finely
    ground
2 sticks (1 cup) unsalted butter,
    softened
1½ cups packed dark brown sugar
2 large eggs
2 teaspoons vanilla extract

LIGHT DOUGH

¾ cup raisins
2 cups sifted all-purpose flour
¼ cup Candied Orange Peel
    (page 120)
¼ teaspoon baking soda
¼ teaspoon salt
1 stick (½ cup) unsalted butter,
    softened
¾ cup granulated sugar
1 large egg
2 tablespoons water
1 teaspoon vanilla extract

A wonderful layered icebox cookie made with a dark dough flavored with chocolate, coffee, nuts, and spices, and a delicate and somewhat sweeter light dough. These colorful and complex-tasting cookies are probably most authentic when chopped red, or red and green, candied cherries are mixed into the light dough. Because the most readily available candied cherries are infused with chemicals, we've substituted our own candied orange rind for them.

Line a 9 × 5 × 3-inch loaf pan: Cut one strip of wax paper 23 inches long and 5 inches wide and use it to line the length of the pan; there should be a 4-inch overhang at each end. Cut another strip of wax paper 21 inches long and 9½ inches wide and use it to line the width of the pan, leaving an overhang of 5 inches at each side.

Make the dark dough: Combine the flour, salt, baking soda, cinnamon, cloves, and instant cappuccino powder in a bowl, stir in the ground nuts and chocolate, and set aside. In a large mixing bowl, cream the butter with an electric mixer until it is light, add the brown sugar, and continue beating until the mixture is very smooth. Add the eggs, one at a time, beating well after each addition, then beat in the vanilla. Add the flour mixture, about 1 cup at a time, and beat until well combined. Set the dough aside while you make the light dough.

Place the raisins in the container of a small (or large) food processor fitted with the steel blade. Sprinkle 1 tablespoon of the flour over the fruit and process until the raisins are finely chopped but not ground, about 1 minute. Transfer the raisins to a mixing bowl. Chop the orange peel by hand and add to the raisins. Add the remaining flour, the baking soda, and salt, and mix well. Reserve. In a large mixing bowl, cream the butter until light, add the granulated sugar, and beat until fluffy. Beat in the egg, then add the water and vanilla. Add the flour mixture one-third at a time, beating well after each addition.

Spread one-half of the dark dough evenly over the bottom of the prepared loaf pan, pressing it firmly into the corners. Cover this layer with all of the light dough, pressing it down and smoothing it out evenly. Spread the remaining dark dough on top of the light dough and smooth out the top. Cover the dough with the wax paper overhang, taping the paper, if necessary, and refrigerate the loaf overnight.

Preheat the oven to 400° F. Use parchment paper to line your cookie sheets to save lots of time. The cookies are so large that only 12 can fit on a large cookie sheet, which means that you'll have to bake them in at least 6 batches.

Remove the loaf pan from the refrigerator and run an icing spatula or a thin-bladed knife around the loaf, separating the wax paper from the pan. Peel back the wax paper flaps on top of the loaf and invert the pan on a cutting board; the loaf should slide out easily. Carefully peel off the wax paper. Cut the loaf in half lengthwise, cover one-half with wax paper, and return it to the refrigerator. Cut the remaining half into crosswise slices ¼ inch thick and arrange the cookies cut-side down on the prepared sheets, leaving about 1½ inches between each cookie. Cut the second half of the loaf the same way. Bake the cookies for 8 minutes, or until they are firm to the touch and the light dough is just beginning to turn golden. Allow the cookies to cool for 1 minute on the sheets (or on the parchment paper), then transfer to racks to cool. Once the cookies have cooled, they can be stored compactly in straight-sided containers with tight-fitting lids at room temperature for up to 1 week or in the freezer for up to 2 months.

BETTY'S LEMON COOKIES

60 TO 65 COOKIES

·

3 cups all-purpose flour
1½ teaspoons baking powder
¼ teaspoon salt
2 sticks (1 cup) unsalted butter,
    softened
½ cup granulated sugar
1 egg, separated
Grated zest of 2 lemons
Juice of ½ lemon
Granulated sugar or colored sugar
    crystals for sprinkling

COOKIE SAMPLER

·

LEMON DROPS
page 39

**JACKIE'S LEMON COCONUT
PECAN BARS**
page 53

BETTY'S LEMON COOKIES
page 74

From Judy's family, these are the cookies she remembers her Aunt Betty making often enough to keep the cookie jar filled, not an easy task in a household of voracious cookie eaters.

Combine the flour, baking powder, and salt on a sheet of wax paper, and set aside. In a mixing bowl, cream the butter with an electric mixer, add the sugar, and beat until light and fluffy. Add the egg yolk, lemon rind, and lemon juice and beat until well mixed. Add the flour mixture and beat well until you have a stiff dough. Turn the dough out on wax paper and form it into rough logs about 1¾ to 2 inches in diameter. Wrap the logs in wax paper and chill for 30 minutes. Shape the logs into even, smooth rolls, rewrap in wax paper, and chill for at least 2 hours or put into freezer bags and freeze.

Preheat the oven to 350° F. Line cookie sheets with parchment paper or butter them. Remove one roll of dough at a time from the refrigerator, slice it ⅛ to ¼ inch thick, and arrange the cookies 1 inch apart on the prepared sheets. Beat the egg white until frothy and brush it on the cookies with a pastry brush. Sprinkle them with granulated sugar or sugar crystals and bake in the middle of the oven for 10 to 13 minutes, or until golden at the edges. Transfer to racks to cool. Store the cookies in airtight containers for up to 1 week, in the freezer for at least 2 months.

If you prefer to cut out fancy shapes, form the dough into flat disks and refrigerate for about an hour, then roll out about ⅛ inch thick and cut into shapes. Bake the rolled cookies for 2 or 3 minutes less than the icebox slices and brush, while barely warm, with Lemon Glaze (page 116), if you like.

GINGER PECAN SLICES

ABOUT 100 COOKIES

■

5 ounces crystallized ginger
2¼ cups all-purpose flour
¼ teaspoon cream of tartar
2 sticks (1 cup) unsalted butter, softened
1 cup confectioners' sugar, sifted
1 large egg
1 cup pecans, chopped

Crystallized ginger and pecans were made for each other. This is an elegant little cookie, gingery and short. You'll find yourself eating quite a few of these in short order.

Place the crystallized ginger in a food processor fitted with the steel blade, sprinkle with 1 tablespoon of the flour, and chop fine. Reserve. On a piece of wax paper, combine the remaining flour and the cream of tartar. In a large bowl, cream the butter and confectioners' sugar with an electric mixer until fluffy, then beat in the egg. Add the flour mixture, beating until smooth. Stir in the pecans and chopped ginger. Divide the dough in half, form each piece into a log about 6½ inches long, and wrap the logs in wax paper. Refrigerate the dough for at least 4 hours, or until firm.

Preheat the oven to 375° F. Line cookie sheets with parchment paper or butter them.

Slice the chilled dough into ⅛-inch slices and place 1 inch apart on the prepared cookie sheets. Bake in the middle of the oven for 8 to 10 minutes, or until the edges just begin to turn golden. Transfer the cookies to wire racks to cool. Store in tightly covered containers for up to 1 week, or freeze for up to 2 months.

PRESSED COOKIES

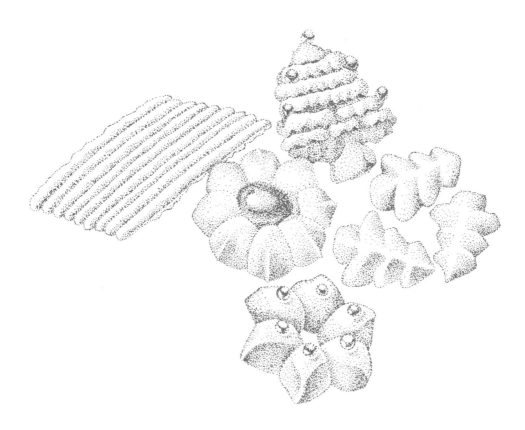

CHARLOTTE'S BUTTER COOKIES *80*

ORANGE OR LEMON BUTTER COOKIES *80*

AUNT MARIE'S CREAM CHEESE COOKIES *81*

MOCHACCINOS *82*

MOTHER GILBERT'S ALMOND SPRITZ COOKIES *83*

PRESSED SPICE COOKIES *84*

Pressed, or spritz, cookies are so impressive looking that it sometimes appears they were turned out by a professional bakery. In fact, a cookie press is a relatively simple mechanism to operate, whether it's a flimsy plastic one with a single setting and only a few disks or a serious Scandinavian model with various thickness settings, 18 disks, and several nozzles; even a novice baker can get the hang of it pretty fast. We've tried three or four brands of presses and found that the Sawa 2000 is the most versatile and easy to use.

When you're deciding what setting and which disks will be most appropriate for your cookie dough, remember that as a rule a stiff dough can be pressed into thinner and more sharply defined shapes than soft dough, which tends to spread and blob out crisp definition.

The baking times and yields for all pressed cookies are variable, depending on the size of the cookie.

CHARLOTTE'S BUTTER COOKIES

ABOUT 80 COOKIES

·

2½ cups all-purpose flour
½ teaspoon baking powder
⅛ teaspoon salt
2 sticks (1 cup) unsalted butter,
   softened
⅔ cup superfine granulated sugar
1 large egg
1½ teaspoons vanilla or almond
   extract

Charlotte Katelvero gives away hundreds of these basic butter cookies every year. The dough can be dropped from a teaspoon or molded into balls, but for Christmas, it's at its dressy best pressed into pretty shapes from a cookie press or a pastry bag. The cookies can be decorated as simply or as ornately as you wish, either before or after baking.

Preheat the oven to 375° F.

Sift the flour, baking powder, and salt onto a sheet of wax paper and set aside. In a large mixing bowl, use an electric mixer to cream the butter until light. Add the sugar and beat until the mixture is fluffy. Beat in the egg and vanilla or almond extract. Add the flour mixture and beat until the dough is smooth.

This dough is firm enough not to lose definition when it's baked. Put it through a cookie press, using the thin setting (if your press has one), pressing out the cookies on an ungreased cookie sheet. You might prefer to pack the dough into a pastry bag fitted with a large or small star tip and pipe out rosettes, wreaths, S-shapes, or any other shape you like. Leave 1 inch between cookies. Bake in the middle of the oven for 8 to 10 minutes, or until the edges are at the point of turning golden. Transfer the cookies to racks to cool. Store in an airtight container for up to 10 days or in the freezer for 2 months.

**ORANGE OR LEMON
BUTTER COOKIES**

Substitute 4 teaspoons of finely grated orange zest or 2 teaspoons of grated lemon zest and 1 or 2 teaspoons of fresh orange or lemon juice for the extract. Decorate before baking with blanched almonds or hazelnuts.

AUNT MARIE'S CREAM CHEESE COOKIES

65 TO 75 COOKIES

■

3 cups sifted all-purpose flour
2 teaspoons baking powder
¼ teaspoon salt
½ cup vegetable shortening
1 stick (½ cup) unsalted butter,
   softened
One 3-ounce package cream
   cheese, softened
1 cup granulated sugar
2 egg yolks
2 teaspoons vanilla extract
1 teaspoon fresh lemon or orange
   juice
Optional decoration: sprinkles,
   dragées, blanched almond
   halves, jam or jelly, or good-
   quality candied fruit

Barbara's Great-aunt Marie was a superb baker, and an endless quantity of treasures seemed to come out of her oven. These rich cookies with the faint tang of cream cheese remind Barbara of Saturday mornings spent baking with Aunt Marie in her kitchen. The recipe makes a soft dough that calls for a thick cookie press setting and strong, simple shapes.

Preheat the oven to 350° F.

Sift the flour, baking powder, and salt into a bowl, and set aside. In a large bowl with an electric mixer, cream the shortening, butter, and cream cheese until light. Gradually add the sugar and continue beating until light and fluffy. Beat in the egg yolks, vanilla, and fruit juice. Add the flour mixture in thirds, beating well after each addition.

Following the manufacturer's instructions, fill a cookie press with the dough and press out shapes on ungreased cookie sheets, leaving about 1½ inches between each cookie. Decorate as you choose. Bake in the middle of the oven for about 13 minutes, or just until slightly tan around the edges. Cool on the cookie sheets for 2 to 3 minutes, then carefully transfer to racks to cool. Store in airtight containers for up to 1 week or in the freezer for up to 2 months.

MOCHACCINOS

∎

*3 ounces bittersweet or semisweet
    chocolate*
*1½ sticks (¾ cup) unsalted butter,
    softened*
¾ cup sifted confectioners' sugar
*¼ cup unsweetened instant
    cappuccino mix or 1½
    tablespoons each instant
    coffee powder and cocoa
    powder*
1 large egg
1 teaspoon vanilla extract
2 cups all-purpose flour
*1 cup pecans, blanched almonds,
    or hazelnuts, finely ground*

DECORATION
BEFORE BAKING: *chocolate shot,
    chocolate-covered coffee
    beans, or mini chocolate
    chips, or*
AFTER BAKING: *6 ounces
    bittersweet or semisweet
    chocolate, melted, and ½ cup
    chopped nuts*

Bittersweet chocolate and instant cappuccino powder make a delicious and sophisticated combination. Although these cookies can be decorated before baking, we much prefer dipping them in melted bittersweet chocolate after they've cooled.

Preheat the oven to 375° F.

Melt the 3 ounces of chocolate in the top of a double boiler or in a small bowl set in a pan of hot water. In a large bowl, cream the butter until light, using an electric mixer, then add the sugar and instant cappuccino and beat until fluffy. Beat in the egg and vanilla. While the melted chocolate is still warm, beat it into the creamed mixture. Add the flour and ground nuts and beat until the dough is well blended and smooth; it will be quite soft.

Press the dough through a cookie press set to a thin setting, following the manufacturer's instructions, or turn the mixture into a pastry bag fitted with a large star tip. Press out cookies on ungreased cookie sheets or pipe out wreaths, curlicues, strips, or any other shape that takes your fancy, leaving 1 inch between each cookie. At this point you can decorate the cookies with any of the "before baking" ingredients suggested. Bake in the middle of the oven for 8 to 10 minutes, or until the cookies are firm and a uniform light mocha color. Transfer them to racks to cool.

If you have not already decorated the cookies, dip each cookie halfway or one-third of the way into the 6 ounces of melted chocolate, scrape the bottom of the cookie against the rim of the pan or bowl of chocolate, then dip the cookie top into the chopped nuts. Place the cookies on a sheet of wax paper to allow the chocolate to harden. Store in an airtight container for up to 2 weeks.

MOTHER GILBERT'S ALMOND SPRITZ COOKIES

ABOUT 60 COOKIES

·

2½ cups sifted all-purpose flour
¼ teaspoon salt
2 sticks (1 cup) unsalted butter, softened
¾ cup granulated sugar
3 egg yolks
¼ cup blanched almonds, finely chopped
½ teaspoon almond extract
Optional decoration: sprinkles, dragées, blanched almond halves, jam or jelly, or good-quality candied fruit

COOKIE SAMPLER

·

SPECULAAS
page 104

MOCHACCINOS
page 82

RENATA'S VANILLA CRESCENTS
page 28

These were Mrs. Gilbert's very special Christmas cookies, and you'll see why as soon as you've eaten one—they're rich and buttery, with a delicate almond flavor. This is a soft dough, and you'll have better results if you use a thicker press setting and clear, uncomplicated shapes. The cookies are very fragile during and after baking, and even after cooling, so handle them gently and pack them with care. They freeze very well.

Preheat the oven to 350° F.

Combine the flour and salt on a piece of wax paper and set aside. In a large bowl, cream the butter with an electric mixer, add the sugar, and continue beating until light and fluffy. Beat in the egg yolks, chopped almonds, and almond extract. Gradually add the flour mixture, beating well after each addition.

Fill a cookie press with the dough, following the manufacturer's instructions, and press cookies onto ungreased cookie sheets, leaving 1½ inches between each cookie. If you like, the cookies can be topped with any of the optional decorations suggested above or with any other suitable decoration before baking. Bake in the middle of the oven for 10 to 13 minutes, or just until the edges are lightly browned. Cool the cookies on the pans for 2 minutes, then carefully transfer them to racks to cool. Store in airtight containers for 1 week or in the freezer for up to 2 months.

PRESSED SPICE COOKIES

ABOUT 75 SMALL COOKIES

2¼ cups sifted all-purpose flour
¼ teaspoon baking soda
1 teaspoon cinnamon
½ teaspoon ground ginger
½ teaspoon allspice
¼ teaspoon ground cloves
¼ teaspoon freshly grated nutmeg
¼ teaspoon salt
1 stick (½ cup) unsalted butter,
    softened
½ cup granulated sugar
1 large egg
¼ cup unsulfured molasses

This is an easily managed dough that you can press out into thin, fancy shapes. Use the Christmas tree disk, if you have one. The crisp, spicy cookies keep very well.

Preheat the oven to 350° F.

In a bowl or on a sheet of wax paper, combine the flour, baking soda, cinnamon, ginger, allspice, cloves, nutmeg, and salt, and set aside. In a large bowl, cream the butter with an electric mixer, add the sugar, and continue beating until the mixture is light and fluffy. Beat in the egg and molasses until well blended. Gradually add the flour mixture, beating well after each addition, until you have a soft, smooth dough.

Following the manufacturer's instructions, fill a cookie press with the dough and press out cookies on ungreased cookie sheets, leaving 1 inch between each cookie. Bake in the middle of the oven for 8 to 10 minutes, or until a rich golden brown. Transfer the cookies to racks to cool. Store in airtight containers at room temperature for 5 to 6 weeks.

ROLLED COOKIES

Rolled cookies offer the holiday baker the widest scope in terms of flavors, textures, shapes, and decorative possibilities—delicate sugar cookies, crisp molasses cookies, melt-in-your-mouth shortbread, decorated gingerbread people, earthy filled oatmeal cookies, and elegant lemon tartlets are just a few of the choices in this chapter.

When it comes to rolling them out, all doughs are not equal, and sometimes the same dough, made with identical ingredients, is not equal to its previous incarnation, depending on the weather. It's better to wait for a dry day before rolling out dough.

As a rule, we find it's easier to roll these doughs on wax paper, sometimes on one sheet, sometimes between two sheets. To keep a single sheet of paper from sliding around on your countertop as you use your rolling pin, tape it down using a piece of masking tape in the middle of each edge of the wax paper (not at the corners, they will just tear off under pressure). Lightly flour the paper and top of the dough, if necessary.

Other doughs are easier to roll out between two loose sheets of wax paper, flouring or not as necessary. This method works well when you want to roll the dough on both sides: after rolling the dough one or two turns on one side, gently lift off the top piece of paper and, if the dough is sticky, lightly flour it again. Replace the wax paper and turn the dough over so that the bottom sheet of paper is now on top. Lift off that sheet and sprinkle the dough with flour, if necessary. Replace the paper and continue rolling out the dough until it is as thin as you want it to be. Remove the top sheet of paper and cut out cookies.

If you're sharing the baking chores with children, you might ask

them to choose the shapes and cut out the cookies. *Always cut cookies beginning at the outer edges of the dough and working your way toward the center.* If the dough has softened by the time the cookies are cut, it's a simple matter to slide the wax paper holding the dough onto a baking sheet and refrigerate it for about 10 minutes, or until the dough is firm enough not to tear when the cookies are removed from the scraps.

For most of the cookie doughs in this chapter, the scraps can be rerolled once; after that, the dough becomes too elastic and toughens as it bakes.

Christmas tree ornaments

To make holes through which string or hooks can be threaded, stick a 1-inch piece of uncooked spaghetti into each cookie before it is baked. Be sure to make the hole at least ¼ inch away from the edge of the cookie. If you want to make a hole large enough to accommodate a piece of decorative ribbon, use a piece of small tubular pasta to make the hole. First use the pasta to punch out a small hole of dough, discard the dough, then put the pasta back into the hole and bake. After baking, remove the spaghetti as soon as you take the cookies out of the oven.

SPICED SHORTBREAD

45 TO 50 MEDIUM COOKIES

2 cups all-purpose flour
1 teaspoon ground cardamom
1 teaspoon ground ginger
½ teaspoon cinnamon
2 sticks (1 cup) unsalted butter, softened
¾ cup packed dark brown sugar
1 teaspoon grated lemon zest

This is one of our favorite cookies; the dough is easy to make, and while it bakes the house is filled with the wonderful aroma of cardamom and ginger. The cookies look great cut into almost any shape, but we especially like to make gaggles of geese, prides of lions, or flights of bats(!), tie them together with festive ribbon, and take them when we visit friends.

On a piece of wax paper, combine the flour, cardamom, ginger, and cinnamon, and set aside. In a large bowl, using an electric mixer, cream the butter until light, add the brown sugar, and continue beating the mixture until fluffy. Beat in the lemon zest, then add the flour mixture in thirds, beating well after each addition. If you are short of time, roll out the dough at once; otherwise, for easier handling, form it into a disk, wrap in wax paper, and refrigerate for about 1 hour.

Preheat the oven to 350° F. Line cookie sheets with parchment paper or butter them. Roll out the dough ¼ inch thick between sheets of wax paper, cut into medium-sized fancy shapes, and place the cookies about 1 inch apart on the prepared sheets. Bake for 12 to 14 minutes, or until just beginning to brown at the edges. Cool the cookies on the baking sheet for 2 minutes, then transfer to racks to cool completely. Store in an airtight container for up to 2 weeks or in the freezer for up to 3 months.

MILLIE'S SUGAR COOKIES

110 TO 120 SMALL COOKIES

2 cups plus 2 tablespoons all-
  purpose flour
Scant ½ teaspoon baking soda
½ teaspoon cream of tartar
1¾ sticks (⅞ cup) unsalted butter,
  softened
6 tablespoons granulated sugar
½ cup confectioners' sugar, sifted
1 large egg
2 teaspoons vanilla extract
Armagnac Glaze (page 116) or
  Cinnamon Sugar (page 120)

COOKIE SAMPLER

■

**MILLIE'S
SUGAR COOKIES**
page 90

**AUNT MARIE'S
PEANUT BUTTER
COOKIES**
page 34

**LEMON-FROSTED
WALNUT BARS**
page 50

Millie Hoffman, who is welcome everywhere on her own merits, often brings a tin of these sugar cookies when she comes to call. The dough is remarkably versatile: It can be put through a cookie press, dropped, molded, or made into icebox cookies. But the rolled cookies, their delicate flavor subtly heightened by a light glaze or a sprinkling of cinnamon sugar, are unquestionably the best. Should you want to shine like Millie, just bring an assortment of plain, lemon, and orange sugar cookies to the next potluck dinner party you attend.

Combine the flour, baking soda, and cream of tartar on a sheet of wax paper and set aside. In a large mixing bowl, cream the butter until light, using an electric mixer, then add the sugars and continue beating until light and very fluffy. Beat in the egg and then the vanilla. Add the flour mixture, one-half at a time, and beat until the dough is smooth and soft. Divide it into 3 pieces and form each into a rectangular disk about ½ inch thick. Wrap the pieces individually in wax paper and refrigerate for at least 2 hours.

Preheat the oven to 375° F. Roll out the dough as thin as possible (⅛ inch, or less) between sheets of wax paper (page 87) and cut out small, fancy shapes. By now, the dough may have softened again, making it difficult to dislodge the cookies from the wax paper. Just slide the sheet of dough, still on the wax paper, onto a baking sheet and refrigerate for 10 minutes. Using an icing spatula, transfer the cookies to an ungreased cookie sheet, leaving 1 inch between each. Refrigerate the scraps as they accumulate and roll them out once. If you are going to finish the cookies with cinnamon sugar, sprinkle them with the sugar before baking.

Bake the cookies in the middle of the oven for 6 to 7 minutes, or until they are lightly colored around the edges.

Leave the cookies on the baking sheet for about 2 minutes, then transfer to a rack to cool. If you are going to glaze the cookies, brush them lightly with the glaze while they are barely warm.

Store in airtight containers for up to 1 week. Layer in stiff freezer containers and freeze for up to 2 months.

LEMON SUGAR COOKIES

Omit the vanilla. After the egg has been beaten into the creamed mixture, add the finely grated rind of 2 lemons and 1 tablespoon of lemon juice. Brush the warm baked cookies with Lemon Glaze (page 116).

ORANGE SUGAR COOKIES

Omit the vanilla. After the egg has been beaten into the creamed mixture, add the finely grated rind of 1 large orange and 1 tablespoon of good-quality orange liqueur. Brush the warm baked cookies with Orange Glaze (page 116).

MOLDED SUGAR COOKIES

Prepare the dough as instructed, form it into a ball, wrap in wax paper, and refrigerate for at least 2 hours. Pinch off pieces of dough and form them into 1-inch balls. Roll the balls in cinnamon sugar, place 1½ inches apart on prepared cookie sheets, and flatten with the bottom of a glass, buttered and dipped in cinnamon sugar. Bake for 8 to 10 minutes, or until the cookies begin to color around the edges.

LINZER WREATHS

18 TO 20 WREATHS

·

1 cup plus 3 tablespoons all-purpose flour
¼ cup granulated sugar
¼ cup packed light brown sugar
2½ cups (9 ounces) finely ground toasted blanched almonds
½ teaspoon cinnamon
¼ teaspoon freshly grated nutmeg
Grated zest of 1 lemon
1 stick (½ cup) cold unsalted butter, cut into 8 pieces, plus cold unsalted butter as needed
Green sugar crystals
½ cup seedless raspberry or currant jam
Sifted confectioners' sugar

COOKIE SAMPLER

·

AUNT MARIE'S THIMBLE COOKIES
page 34

LINZER WREATHS
page 92

AUNT ETHEL'S CREAM CHEESE COOKIES
page 103

Linzer torte is a renowned, mildly spiced, butter-rich Viennese pastry that's usually made with a lattice crust.

The dough for this cookie version of the torte is easily made in the food processor. Unlike the original Linzer torte dough, this one does not contain egg; nevertheless, it's still a little tricky to roll out, even between sheets of wax paper.

Sprinkled with green sugar crystals, the cookies look like festive Christmas wreaths but, if you prefer, a simple dusting of confectioners' sugar will do just as nicely.

In the bowl of a food processor fitted with the steel blade, place the flour, sugars, almonds, cinnamon, nutmeg, and grated lemon zest. Pulse 2 or 3 times to blend well. Distribute the butter on top of the flour mixture and pulse 5 times, then process for 2 minutes, or until the dough starts to form into large clumps. If the mixture is too crumbly to form a dough, add cold butter, 1 teaspoon at a time, and process.

Divide the dough in half, form into disks, and wrap in wax paper. Refrigerate the dough for 45 minutes.

Preheat the oven to 325° F.

Place a piece of dough on a sheet of wax paper that has been taped to the work surface and roll it out ⅛ inch thick. Cut out rounds with a scalloped 2½-inch cookie cutter. Using a 1-inch cutter, cut out rounds from the centers of half the cookies to make the tops of the wreaths. Gather up the scraps of dough into a disk, wrap in wax paper, and refrigerate. Sprinkle the sugar crystals lightly over the wreath tops and carefully transfer all the cookies (tops and bases separately, not assembled) to an ungreased cookie sheet. Bake 10 to 13 minutes, or until lightly colored. Cool the cookies in the pan. Continue making cookies with the remaining dough.

Spread each plain round with jam. Dust the wreath tops with confectioners' sugar and press them over the jam-covered rounds to form sandwiches. Store the cookies in

airtight containers, separated by sheets of wax paper, for 2 days in the refrigerator and up to 2 months in the freezer.

If you choose to freeze the cookies, you'll find that they taste delicious while they're still frozen.

SHORTBREAD

25 TO 30 LARGE COOKIES

1⅞ sticks (15 tablespoons)
   unsalted butter, softened
½ cup granulated sugar
½ teaspoon grated lemon zest
½ teaspoon vanilla extract
2 cups cake flour

Just what you'd expect—rich, buttery cookies that melt in your mouth. It's a challenge to stop eating these once you start.

With an electric mixer, cream the butter until light in a large mixing bowl. Add the sugar and beat until the mixture is fluffy and light. Beat in the lemon zest and vanilla, then add the flour and beat well. Turn the dough out on a piece of wax paper, form it into a disk, and refrigerate for 1 hour, until firm enough to roll out.

Preheat the oven to 325° F. Line cookie sheets with parchment paper or butter them.

Roll out the dough ¼ inch thick and cut into large fancy shapes. Place on the prepared baking sheets about 1½ inches apart and bake in the middle of the oven for 16 to 18 minutes, or until firm and very faintly colored around the edges. Let cool for 2 to 3 minutes on the baking sheets, then carefully transfer to racks to cool. These cookies are quite fragile, so handle them gently. Store in airtight containers for up to 2 weeks or in the freezer for up to 2 months.

FILLED GINGER COOKIES

■

DATE-NUT FILLING

1 pound chopped pitted dates
½ cup granulated sugar
½ cup hot water
1 cup chopped walnuts
1 teaspoon vanilla extract

FIG FILLING

1 cup ground figs
1 teaspoon grated lemon zest
1 tablespoon fresh lemon juice
½ cup granulated sugar
2 tablespoons flour
1 cup hot water

GINGER COOKIE DOUGH

2¾ cups all-purpose flour
½ teaspoon baking soda
1 teaspoon baking powder
2 teaspoons ground ginger
½ teaspoon freshly grated nutmeg
¼ teaspoon salt
1 stick (½ cup) unsalted butter,
   softened
½ cup granulated sugar
½ cup packed dark brown sugar
1 large egg
½ cup sour cream

A terrific snack cookie—they're especially satisfying, although not necessarily nutritionally complete, for breakfast. During baking they puff up and look like fat little empanadas. If you prefer a crisper cookie, roll the dough as thin as you can without tearing it. For those who like a softer, more cakelike cookie, ⅛ of an inch or a little thicker is just right. Either of these fillings is rich and delicious. We've used the leftovers for filling tartlets and sandwiches and as a breakfast spread—a great combination with cream cheese.

To make the date-nut filling, combine the dates, sugar, and water in a heavy saucepan and cook over moderate heat, stirring constantly, until thick, about 5 minutes. This mixture burns easily, so be vigilant. Let the filling cool, then stir in the nuts and vanilla.

To make the fig filling, combine the figs, lemon rind and juice, sugar, flour, and hot water in a medium saucepan and cook over moderate heat, stirring often, until the mixture is thick, about 10 minutes. Cool the filling.

To make the cookie dough, combine the flour, baking soda, baking powder, ginger, nutmeg, and salt on a sheet of wax paper and set aside. Cream the butter in a large mixing bowl with an electric mixer, add the sugars, and continue beating until light and fluffy. Add the egg and beat until well mixed. Add the flour mixture and sour cream alternately in thirds, beating well after each addition. The dough will be very soft. Turn it out on the countertop and with lightly floured hands form it into 2 balls. Flatten the dough into disks, wrap in wax paper, and refrigerate for at least 3 hours, or until the dough is firm enough to roll out.

Preheat the oven to 350° F. Line cookie sheets with parchment paper or grease them.

Roll out the dough between lightly floured sheets of

wax paper to a scant ⅛ inch thickness. Cut the dough into 2½-inch rounds. Place a rounded teaspoon of filling in the centers of half of the dough rounds. Top with the remaining rounds, press the filling down lightly, and seal the edges with the tines of a fork.

Place the cookies on the prepared sheets, leaving 1½ inches between each one, and bake for 12 to 14 minutes, or until golden. Transfer to racks to cool. Store the cookies in tightly covered containers for up to 10 days or in the freezer for up to 2 months.

DATE-FILLED OATMEAL COOKIES

ABOUT **45** COOKIES

∎

2 cups old-fashioned rolled oats
2¼ cups all-purpose flour
1¼ teaspoons baking soda
½ teaspoon salt
2 teaspoons cinnamon
½ cup vegetable shortening
1 stick (½ cup) unsalted butter,
    softened
1 cup packed dark brown sugar
2 large eggs
2 teaspoons vanilla extract
1 recipe Date-Nut Filling (page 94)

COOKIE SAMPLER

∎

**DOUBLE CHOCOLATE
GINGER MACADAMIA
COOKIES**
page 39

**AUNT MARIE'S
CREAM CHEESE
COOKIES**
page 81

**DATE-FILLED
OATMEAL COOKIES**
page 96

Another cookie jar favorite, these were adapted from an old Vermont recipe given to us by our friend Janet Gilbert. They have an earthy texture and flavor, and the oats taste especially good with the date filling.

Combine the oats, flour, baking soda, salt, and cinnamon in a bowl or on a large piece of wax paper. Cream the shortening and butter in a large mixing bowl using an electric mixer, add the brown sugar, and continue beating until well combined. Add the eggs one at a time, beating well after each addition, then beat in the vanilla. Add the oat mixture one-third at a time and beat well, using your hands for the final mixing. The dough will be soft. Divide it into quarters and form each piece into a disk. Wrap the disks in wax paper and chill for at least 1 hour.

Preheat the oven to 375° F. Line cookie sheets with parchment paper or butter them.

Roll out the dough ⅛ inch thick between sheets of unfloured wax paper, lifting the paper and turning the dough as described on page 87. Discard the top piece of wax paper, cut the dough into 3-inch rounds, and smush down a heaping teaspoon of the filling over half of each circle. By now the dough will be quite soft again, and it will be difficult to separate the cookies from the scraps, so slide the wax paper with the cutout cookies still on it onto a baking sheet and refrigerate for about 10 minutes. Remove from the refrigerator and, with an icing spatula, remove the scraps and fold the unfilled halves of the cookie rounds over the filling, making half-moon shapes, and press the edges to seal. Crimp the edges with a fork and place the cookies 1½ inches apart on the prepared sheets. Bake in the middle of the oven for 10 to 12 minutes, or until golden brown. Transfer the cookies to racks to cool. Store in airtight containers for up to 3 weeks; freeze in freezer bags for up to 2 months.

BUTTER HORNS

48 COOKIES

•

2 cups all-purpose flour
¼ teaspoon salt
2 sticks (1 cup) unsalted butter,
    cut into 8 pieces
1 egg yolk
¾ cup sour cream

FILLING
1 cup finely chopped nuts
1 cup dried fruit: chopped
    apricots, figs, or dates, or
    whole dried currants
¼ cup Cinnamon Sugar
    (page 120)
2 tablespoons grated orange zest

6 tablespoons honey

A soft sour cream dough is drizzled with honey, sprinkled with fruit and nuts, and then cut into wedges, which are rolled up into tiny horn shapes. Our favorite filling combinations are apricots and almonds, figs or dates and walnuts, and currants and pecans. The recipe for these delicious cookies came from the files of Mary Garrity's grandmother.

Put the flour and salt into the bowl of a food processor fitted with the steel blade and distribute the butter over the top of the flour. Pulse the machine until the mixture resembles coarse meal. In a cup, stir the egg yolk and sour cream just to blend, then pour over the flour mixture. Run the machine until a soft, sticky dough forms around the shaft. Turn the dough out onto a sheet of wax paper, and divide it into thirds. Shape each piece into a ball, dust lightly with flour, and wrap in wax paper. Refrigerate overnight.

Preheat the oven to 350° F. It's best to use parchment paper to line the cookie sheets, since the filling leaks out of the cookies as they bake, making the pans difficult to clean.

Make the filling or fillings: In a small bowl combine the nuts, chopped fruit, cinnamon sugar, and orange zest. Reserve.

Roll out one ball of dough at a time into a circle ⅛ inch thick. Trim the dough into a 9-inch circle, reserving the scraps. Drizzle 1½ tablespoons of honey evenly over the dough, then sprinkle with one-quarter of the filling. Cut into 12 wedges, roll up each wedge from the wide end, and place the horns about 1 inch apart on the prepared sheets. Repeat with the other pieces of dough, using the scraps to roll out a fourth round. Bake in the middle of the oven for 21 to 23 minutes, or until golden brown. Transfer to racks to cool. Store in airtight containers for up to 4 days at room temperature or for 1 week in the refrigerator. The cookies can be frozen for up to 2 months.

LEBKUCHEN

18 TO 20 GINGERBREAD PEOPLE ABOUT 5 INCHES TALL

▪

4 to 4½ cups all-purpose flour
1½ teaspoons baking powder
    (substitute baking soda if you
    use molasses instead of honey)
½ teaspoon freshly grated nutmeg
½ teaspoon ground ginger
½ teaspoon ground cloves
1 teaspoon cinnamon
½ stick (¼ cup) unsalted butter,
    softened
¾ cup granulated sugar
1 large egg
1 egg yolk
1¼ teaspoons vanilla extract
¼ cup honey or unsulfured
    molasses
1½ tablespoons half and
    half cream
Dried currants
Red hots
Decorator's Icing (page 117),
    optional

These are mildly sweet, fragrantly spiced cookies, quite dense in texture. They start out as a stiff dough and finish as sturdy cookies. Lebkuchen keep well, and in fact their flavor improves with time. Honey keeps these cookies light in color; molasses will darken their color and deepen their flavor.

Preheat the oven to 350° F. Line cookie sheets with parchment paper or butter them.

On a piece of wax paper, combine 4 cups of the flour with the baking powder (or baking soda, if you are using molasses), and spices. In a large bowl, use an electric mixer to cream the butter and sugar until light and fluffy. Beat in the egg, egg yolk, and vanilla, then add the honey or molasses and the half and half, beating until smooth. Add the flour mixture in thirds, beating well after each addition. The dough should be quite stiff, but should hold together if you pinch a bit between your fingers. If the dough is sticky, beat in the remaining ½ cup of flour.

Using a light dusting of flour to keep the dough from sticking, roll out the dough between pieces of wax paper (page 87) until it is a scant ¼ inch thick. Using a cookie cutter, cut the dough into gingerbread people or any other shapes you like. Transfer the cookies to the prepared baking sheets, leaving 2 inches between each one, and decorate them, using dried currants for eyes and red hots for buttons. Bake in the middle of the oven for 8 minutes, or until lightly browned. Transfer the cookies to wire racks to cool. When cool, pipe on decorator's icing if desired. Store in an airtight container for up to 4 weeks.

CINNAMON PASTRY CRUST STARS

15 TO 18 MEDIUM STARS

·

1 cup all-purpose flour
¼ cup packed light brown sugar
1 teaspoon cinnamon
1 stick (½ cup) unsalted butter,
   cut into 8 pieces
Cinnamon Sugar (page 120)

These are simple, sophisticated, tasty little cookies. They're crisp, buttery, cinnamon-scented, and easy to make. This recipe can be doubled easily.

Preheat the oven to 350° F. Line cookie sheets with parchment paper or butter them.

Using a food processor or electric mixer, combine the flour, brown sugar, and cinnamon. Arrange the butter over the top and process until the mixture forms a smooth dough. Pat the dough into a ball and place it on a large sheet of wax paper. Lightly flour a rolling pin and roll out the dough ⅛ inch thick. Use a medium star cookie cutter (or any shape you like) to cut out cookies and place them 1 inch apart on the prepared sheets. Sprinkle the cookies with cinnamon sugar and bake in the middle of the oven for 10 to 12 minutes, or until the cookies are golden. Transfer immediately to wire racks to cool. Store carefully in airtight containers for up to 1 week or in the freezer for up to 2 months.

For a festive look, put red hots or silver dragées on cookies before baking. After baking, cool the cookies, then dip the points of the stars in Chocolate Dipping Glaze (page 118) or, for iced stars, dip the points in your favorite flavored confectioners' sugar glaze (pages 116 through 118).

COOKIE SAMPLER

·

MOTHER GILBERT'S CHOCOLATE COOKIES

ABOUT 80 COOKIES

•

3 cups all-purpose flour
1½ teaspoons baking soda
¼ teaspoon salt
½ teaspoon cinnamon
½ teaspoon ground cloves
½ teaspoon freshly grated nutmeg
1 stick (½ cup) unsalted butter,
   softened
½ cup granulated sugar
½ cup unsulfured molasses
1 large egg
4 ounces unsweetened chocolate,
   melted and cooled
1 tablespoon hot tap water
Decorator's Icing (page 117)

This Gilbert family recipe produces thin, crisp cookies with a deep chocolatey taste that's intensified by molasses and spices. Cut into fancy shapes and decorated with icing and sprinkles, they make a particularly appealing gift. Roll out and bake the cookies on a cool, dry day.

On a sheet of wax paper, combine the flour, baking soda, salt, cinnamon, cloves, and nutmeg, and set aside. In a large mixing bowl, cream the butter with an electric mixer, add the sugar, and beat until very well combined. Add the molasses and egg and beat well. Stir in the chocolate, then beat in the hot water. Add the flour mixture in thirds, beating well after each addition. Divide the dough into 3 or 4 pieces, form them into balls, and flatten them into disks. Wrap the dough in wax paper and refrigerate for at least 2 hours, or until firm.

Preheat the oven to 350° F. Line cookie sheets with parchment paper or butter them.

Roll out the dough between 2 sheets of wax paper until it is ⅛ inch thick, or less. Cut the dough into fancy shapes and transfer the cookies carefully to the prepared baking sheets, leaving about 1 inch between each. Bake in the middle of the oven for 8 to 10 minutes, or until the cookies are just firm. Transfer to racks to cool.

Pipe the icing over the cookies in decorative patterns or outlines, or drip it from a spoon. Allow the icing to harden before storing the cookies. Keep for up to 2 weeks in an airtight container. The cookies do not freeze well.

ENGLISH SPICE COOKIES

50 TO 60 COOKIES

3¼ cups all-purpose flour
1 teaspoon baking soda
1 teaspoon cinnamon
1 teaspoon ground cloves
½ teaspoon freshly grated nutmeg
¼ teaspoon salt
1 stick (½ cup) unsalted butter, softened
1 cup granulated sugar
1 large egg
½ cup sour cream
1 cup currants, plus currants for decoration

These mildly spiced cookies are a pale creamy tan and dotted with currants. The dough is very easy to roll out and cut into silly (or serious) shapes. Ask kids to help you choose the shapes, cut them out, and then decorate the tops with more currants.

Combine the flour, baking soda, cinnamon, cloves, nutmeg, and salt on a sheet of wax paper and set aside. In a large mixing bowl, cream the butter using an electric mixer, add the sugar, and beat until light and fluffy. Add the egg and beat well. Beat in the sour cream and 1 cup of currants. Add the flour mixture in thirds, beating well after each addition. Turn the dough out on the counter and divide into 3 or 4 pieces. Form each piece into a disk, wrap in wax paper, and refrigerate for about 2 hours, or until firm enough to roll out.

Preheat the oven to 350° F. Line cookie sheets with parchment paper or butter them.

Roll out the dough ¼ to ⅛ inch thick, cut into shapes, and decorate with more currants, if you like. Place the cookies on the prepared sheets about 1¼ inches apart and bake in the middle of the oven for 10 to 13 minutes, or until just golden around the edges. Transfer to racks to cool. Store the cookies in an airtight container for 3 weeks or in the freezer for up to 3 months.

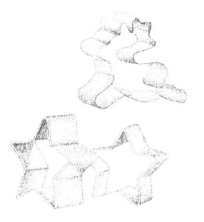

PEPPARKAKOR COOKIES

48 TO 60 COOKIES

■

1¾ cups all-purpose flour
½ teaspoon baking soda
Pinch of salt
1 teaspoon cinnamon
¾ teaspoon ground ginger
½ teaspoon ground cloves
¼ teaspoon freshly grated nutmeg
½ stick (¼ cup) unsalted butter, softened
6 tablespoons granulated sugar
½ egg (break egg into measuring cup, stir with a fork to combine yolk and white, divide mixture in half)
6 tablespoons unsulfured molasses
½ teaspoon grated lemon zest
½ teaspoon grated orange zest
Decorator's Icing (page 117)

These dark, spicy cookies are our first choice as Christmas tree ornaments, and they are delicious to eat as well. When made to decorate the tree, the cookies should be very crisp, so take care not to underbake them.

On a piece of wax paper, combine the flour, baking soda, salt, cinnamon, ginger, cloves, and nutmeg. In a large mixing bowl, use an electric mixer to cream the butter and sugar until light and fluffy. Add the half egg and beat until smooth. Add the molasses and grated rinds and beat until well combined. Add the flour mixture in thirds, beating well after each addition. Divide the dough in half, form each half into a round, and wrap in wax paper and then in foil or plastic wrap. Refrigerate for 8 hours or overnight.

Preheat the oven to 375° F. Line cookie sheets with parchment paper or butter them. Remove one piece of dough from the refrigerator (leave the other half in the refrigerator until you are ready to use it). Roll out the dough ⅛ inch thick between sheets of wax paper (page 87), lightly flouring the dough if necessary. Cut the dough into decorative shapes and arrange the cookies about 1 inch apart on the prepared sheets. If you wish to use the cookies as Christmas tree ornaments, see page 88 for instructions. Bake in the middle of the oven for 6 to 8 minutes, or until lightly browned. Transfer the cookies to racks to cool. When the cookies have cooled completely, decorate with icing.

Store in airtight containers for up to 4 weeks.

AUNT ETHEL'S CREAM CHEESE COOKIES

ABOUT 100 COOKIES

∎

1 pound all-purpose flour
1 teaspoon salt
4 sticks (1 pound) unsalted butter,
*   cut into 32 pieces*
Two 8-ounce packages (1 pound)
*   cream cheese, cut into 16*
*   pieces*
Generous ½ cup best-quality jam
*   or preserves, or Date-Nut*
*   Filling (page 94)*
Vanilla Confectioners' Sugar
*   (page 119)*

COOKIE SAMPLER
∎

**AUNT ETHEL'S
CREAM CHEESE
COOKIES**
page 103

**OATMEAL CURRANT
COOKIES**
page 21

PECAN BALLS
page 30

Barbara's Aunt Ethel has been making these little treats for years, and everybody loves them—so much, in fact, that she's been asked repeatedly to make them larger. But Ethel thinks they're perfect just the way she's always made them, and we agree. The sugarless cream cheese dough puffs up in layers, and it's a perfect package for a sweet fruit filling, as well as being a good tartlet crust (see page 108). You'll need a scale to measure the flour for this recipe. You can cut the recipe in half, or even into quarters, if you like.

Preheat the oven to 375° F. Line cookie sheets with parchment paper or butter them.

Put the flour and salt into the bowl of a food processor fitted with the metal blade, then distribute the pieces of butter and cream cheese over the flour. Pulse 4 or 5 times to mix, then process until a smooth dough is formed. Turn the dough onto a piece of wax paper, divide it into thirds, pat each piece into a ball, and dust with flour. Wrap 2 pieces of dough in wax paper and refrigerate.

Roll out the remaining piece of dough a scant ⅛ inch thick on a floured surface, or on wax paper (our preference). With a sharp knife, cut the dough into 2-inch squares. Place ¼ teaspoon of jam in the center of each square. Moisten 2 diagonally opposite corners of each square with water or milk and pinch them together, forming a diamond-shaped envelope for the filling. Place the cookies on the prepared sheets about 1½ inches apart. Repeat with the remaining dough. Bake in the middle of the oven for 10 to 13 minutes, or until puffed and lightly browned. Watch carefully after 10 minutes to see that the cookies don't burn. Transfer to racks and dust with vanilla confectioners' sugar while the cookies are still hot.

Store in an airtight container at room temperature for 2 or 3 days. The cookies are at their best a day or two after they're baked.

SPECULAAS

90 TO 100 COOKIES

3⅓ cups all-purpose flour
2 teaspoons cinnamon
½ teaspoon ground cloves
½ teaspoon ground cardamom
½ teaspoon freshly grated nutmeg
1½ sticks (¾ cup) unsalted butter,
    softened
1½ cups granulated sugar
1 large egg
2½ tablespoons half and
    half cream
1 tablespoon grated lemon zest
1 egg white, beaten until frothy
Granulated sugar or sugar crystals
Sliced natural almonds

Speculaas are crisp, hard, spicy cookies that will remind you of the Dutch windmill cookies your mother bought for you when you were a child. The dough should be rolled out only once, so it is cut with a knife instead of with cookie cutters, which would leave too many scraps. The dough also lends itself to springerle shapes, and instructions for using a springerle rolling pin follow the main recipe.

Combine the flour, cinnamon, cloves, cardamom, and nutmeg on a sheet of wax paper. In a large mixing bowl, cream the butter with an electric mixer, add the sugar, and continue beating until light. Beat in the egg, half and half, and lemon zest. Add the flour mixture gradually and beat until the dough is smooth. Divide the dough in half, form each piece into a disk, wrap in wax paper, and refrigerate until firm but not rock-hard, about 1 hour.

Preheat the oven to 350° F. Line cookie sheets with parchment paper or butter them.

Roll out the dough ⅛ inch thick, brush it all over with the beaten egg white, then sprinkle with sugar. With a sharp knife, cut the dough into 2-inch rectangles, squares, or diamonds. Press an almond slice into the center of each shape. With a large icing spatula, transfer the cookies to the prepared sheets, placing them about ½ inch apart. Bake in the middle of the oven for 10 to 13 minutes, or until the edges just start to brown. Transfer to racks to cool. Store in airtight containers for up to 4 weeks.

**SPRINGERLE-
PATTERNED
SPECULAAS**

With a regular rolling pin, roll the dough out slightly thicker than ⅛ inch. Use a springerle rolling pin to roll out the dough one last time, flattening it out until it is ⅛ inch thick. Brush with beaten egg white and sprinkle with sugar as described above, then, with a sharp knife, cut out cookies following the outlines made by the rolling pin. Do not decorate with almonds. Bake as directed.

MORAVIAN MOLASSES COOKIES

65 TO 85 COOKIES, DEPENDING ON SIZE

3½ cups all-purpose flour
1 teaspoon baking soda
1 teaspoon cinnamon
1 teaspoon ground allspice
1 teaspoon ground ginger
½ teaspoon freshly grated nutmeg
1 stick (½ cup) unsalted butter,
    softened
½ cup packed dark brown sugar
¾ cup unsulfured molasses
Decorator's Icing (page 117),
    optional

COOKIE SAMPLER

SPECULAAS
page 104

PFEFFERNÜSSE
page 33

SPICED SHORTBREAD
page 89

PRESSED
SPICE COOKIES
page 84

Thin and crisp, with a definite but not overwhelming molasses flavor, these cookies taste better every day you can manage to keep them around. This dough is not "forgiving"; it doesn't smooth out during baking. So if there's a blemish on the surface when the cookies go into the oven, it will be there when they come out. But who cares?

Sift the flour, baking soda, cinnamon, allspice, ginger, and nutmeg into a bowl and set aside. In a large mixing bowl, cream the butter with an electric mixer, add the brown sugar, and continue beating until the mixture is light and fluffy. Beat in the molasses. Add the flour mixture, one-third at a time, beating well after each addition. Turn the dough out on the counter and form it into a cohesive mass. It's easiest to roll out the dough in small amounts, so divide it into 5 or 6 pieces, form them into balls, and flatten the balls into disks. Wrap the disks individually in wax paper and refrigerate overnight.

Preheat the oven to 350° F. Line cookie sheets with parchment paper or butter them lightly.

Flour your work surface and rolling pin lightly, then roll out the dough, one piece at a time, as thin as possible, ¹⁄₁₆ to ⅛ inch thick, using only enough flour to keep the dough from sticking. Cut out the dough in small to medium fancy shapes—not too fancy, though. Because the dough is so thin and sticky, it's easier to transfer small, compact cookies to the baking sheet. Using an icing spatula, carefully loosen the cookies from the work surface and place them on the prepared sheets about ¾ inch apart. Refrigerate the scraps and roll out once. Bake for 6 to 10 minutes, or until the cookies are brown all over, but not dark at the edges. Cool on the cookie sheets for about 2 minutes, then transfer to racks to cool completely. If you like, pipe icing on the cookies. Allow the icing to dry before storing the cookies in airtight containers for 2 to 3 months.

PÂTE BRISÉE

ENOUGH FOR 9 TARTLETS

·

1½ cups all-purpose flour
¼ teaspoon salt
¼ teaspoon granulated sugar
½ teaspoon cinnamon
1 teaspoon grated lemon zest
5½ tablespoons cold unsalted
*   butter, cut into 5 pieces*
3 tablespoons cold vegetable
*   shortening, cut into 3 pieces*
¼ cup ice water

Pâte brisée is a snap to make in the food processor. Be sure that the butter and shortening are well chilled.

Place the flour, salt, sugar, cinnamon, and lemon zest in the bowl of a food processor fitted with the steel blade and pulse 2 or 3 times to mix. Arrange the butter and shortening on top of the flour mixture and process until the mixture resembles cornmeal. With the motor running, pour the ice water through the feed tube and process until a soft dough forms. Turn out on a sheet of wax paper, pat into a flat disk, and refrigerate for 2 hours, or until the dough is firm enough to roll out. If you like, you can store the dough, sealed in a heavy plastic bag, for up to 4 days in the refrigerator.

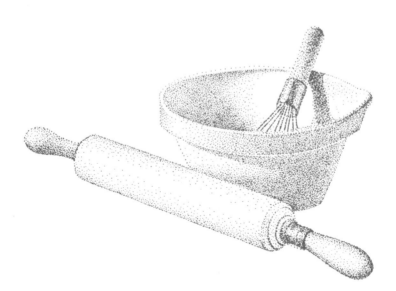

HOLIDAY TARTLETS

18 TARTLETS

2 recipes Pâte Brisée (page 106)
  or ⅓ recipe of dough for Aunt
  Ethel's Cream Cheese
  Cookies (page 103)
1⅔ cups cooked cranberry sauce,
  mincemeat (reconstituted
  condensed mincemeat is fine),
  or Date-Nut Filling
  (page 94), or use several
  fillings

COOKIE SAMPLER

**CINNAMON ORANGE
COCONUT COOKIES**
page 41

HOLIDAY TARTLETS
page 107

**ENGLISH
SPICE COOKIES**
page 101

For this group of tartlets, the filling is topped with a decorative dough cutout and baked in the tartlet shell. The fillings suggested can be made from scratch or, more likely, left over from other recipes or holiday meals. Of course, any thick, chopped fruit compote would be suitable. Homemade chunky applesauce with chopped walnuts or pearsauce made with crystallized ginger would each be a good choice.

Preheat the oven to 425° F.

Divide the dough in half. On a lightly floured surface, roll out one piece of pâte brisée or cream cheese dough ⅛ inch thick. Cut into nine 3-inch rounds and pat them into 3-inch tartlet forms. From the same dough, cut out 9 small stars, circles, hearts, or any other small shape that appeals to you, and set aside for the decoration.

Spoon about 1½ tablespoons of filling into each tart shell and top with a decorative pastry shape. Repeat with the remaining dough and filling. Bake in the middle of the oven for about 30 minutes, or until the crust is golden brown. Cool in the pans for about 10 minutes, then transfer the tartlets to racks to cool.

Serve the tartlets at room temperature. If you plan to keep them for several days before serving, or giving, arrange them on a baking sheet and cover with plastic wrap.

SWEET CREAM CHEESE PASTRY TARTLET SHELLS

9 TARTLET SHELLS

1½ cups plus 2 tablespoons sifted
  all-purpose flour
1 teaspoon baking powder
½ cup granulated sugar
Pinch of salt
1 egg yolk
1 teaspoon vanilla extract
½ teaspoon fresh lemon or
  orange juice
¼ cup vegetable shortening
½ stick (¼ cup) unsalted butter,
  softened
1½ ounces (half of a 3-ounce
  package) cream cheese,
  softened

This is a sweeter dough than pâte brisée or the cream cheese dough in Aunt Ethel's cookies, and it's very easy to roll out and bake before filling.

Place the flour, baking powder, sugar, and salt in the bowl of a food processor and pulse 2 or 3 times to mix. Combine the egg yolk, vanilla, and citrus juice in a cup and stir with a fork just to mix. Add the shortening, butter, and cream cheese to the flour mixture, sprinkle with the egg yolk mixture, and process until a soft dough forms. Turn the dough out on a sheet of wax paper and form into a round, flat disk. Wrap in the paper and refrigerate for 2 hours, or until firm enough to roll out. The dough can be stored, sealed in a heavy plastic bag, in the refrigerator for up to 4 days.

Preheat the oven to 350° F. On a lightly floured surface, roll out the dough a scant ⅛ inch thick. Cut it into 3-inch rounds, transfer them to tartlet pans, and prick the bottoms with a fork in several places. Bake in the middle of the oven for 12 to 15 minutes, or until the shells are golden brown. Cool in the pans for about 3 minutes, then transfer to racks. Fill the shells when they are completely cool.

AUNT ETHEL'S BAKED CREAM CHEESE TARTLET SHELLS

For beautiful, puffy baked tartlet shells, roll out the dough for Aunt Ethel's Cream Cheese Cookies (page 103) as described above and bake for the same length of time as the sweet dough.

JAM OR LEMON TARTLETS

18 TARTLETS

．

18 baked Sweet Cream Cheese
  Pastry Tartlet Shells (page
  108) or Aunt Ethel's Baked
  Cream Cheese Tartlet Shells
  (page 108)
1⅔ cups best-quality jam,
  preserves, or Lemon Curd
  (below)
Confectioners' sugar

An assortment of tartlets makes a pretty dessert for a holiday buffet. These and the Holiday Tartlets on page 107 make sumptuous gifts. Of course, you can't send them through the mail, but neatly and carefully packed in a shallow box, they're easy to take in person.

Fill each tartlet with about 1½ tablespoons of jam or lemon curd. Sift confectioners' sugar over the tops. Serve cold.

LEMON CURD

MAKES 2 CUPS

．

1 cup sugar
8 egg yolks
Generous ½ cup fresh lemon juice
2 teaspoons grated lemon zest
1 stick (½ cup) unsalted butter,
  cut into 8 pieces

Lemon curd is an English teatime favorite as a spread for toast and scones. It also makes a superb filling for tartlets, by itself, as in this recipe, or folded into whipped cream.

In the top of a double boiler, combine the sugar and egg yolks. Place over barely simmering water and stir in the lemon juice and zest. Cook, stirring constantly, until the mixture is warm, then add the butter, one piece at a time, stirring until each piece is incorporated before adding the next. Continue cooking and stirring the curd until it is very thick. Transfer the mixture to a bowl, cover the surface with plastic wrap, and let it cool to room temperature. Chill the curd and use it to fill tartlets or as a spread for bread and muffins. Store in a tightly covered container in the refrigerator for up to 2 weeks.

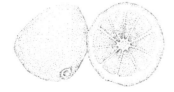

TRIMMING THE CHRISTMAS COOKIES

Decorating is fun, and you don't have to be an artist to turn out beautiful Christmas cookies. Most cookies look wonderful hot out of the oven and need nothing more than the simplest embellishment to dress them up. If you're planning to bake a variety of cookies and want to have some basic decorating staples on hand to use as your mood and creativity dictate, here are some suggestions:

CONFECTIONERS' SUGAR GLAZE

Cookie glazes and icings require few basic ingredients, and they are quick and easy to make. You'll find recipes for some of our favorites in the pages that follow, but you can easily invent your own recipes when you become familiar with the procedures for making them. The ingredients you'll need are confectioners' sugar, lemon and orange juice, flavored extracts, egg whites, spirits, and food colorings.

Confectioners' sugar is the building block for most glazes. Mix ¼ cup of confectioners' sugar with 1 tablespoon of water and you'll have a spreadable glaze. Add more water, a few drops at a time, and the glaze will be thin enough to drizzle freely over your cookies. A sugar-and-water glaze may be flavored easily with the addition of an extract. Vanilla and almond extracts are used most often, but try more unusual flavorings such as anise, peppermint, orange, or lemon. Extracts are intensely flavored, so add them drop by drop, tasting as you go.

Now go back to your ¼ cup of confectioner's sugar. Instead of water, add a tablespoon of fresh lemon juice, and you'll have a delicious, tart lemon glaze that will complement almost any cookie. Grate a little lemon zest into the glaze, or substitute orange juice for the lemon juice.

You can make a most sophisticated glaze by mixing confectioners' sugar with spirits. We've used Armagnac, Grand Marnier, brandy, cognac, anisette, and rum with great success.

•

Some glazes are used for their appearance, but others, especially thin glazes, are meant to be tasted and not seen. All glazes should be lightly

brushed on the cookies while they are still warm, but not hot. If the glaze is put on hot cookies, the part of the cookie underneath the glaze will become soggy.

Glazes are easy to apply with a feather or pastry brush. Or dip the tops or ends of the cookies into the mixture. Glaze also can be drizzled from a spoon in a decorative pattern over the tops of the cookies.

■

CHOCOLATE GLAZE (page 118) is a painless way to give cookies an elegant finish, which can be further enhanced by dipping the glazed part of the cookies into finely chopped nuts.

■

DECORATOR'S ICING (page 117) is used for ornament rather than flavor. Its basic ingredients, confectioners' sugar and egg whites, are combined into a thick, smooth icing that is opaque and dries quickly. The ratio of sugar to egg whites is important, so it's a good idea to follow the recipe and not experiment on your own unless you are an experienced cook. We use decorator's icing to outline cutout cookies, and to make features such as eyes, hair, buttons, and so on for gingerbread people and wild beasts. There are three ways of piping decorator's icing onto cookies:

1. A pastry bag fitted with a small writing (plain) tip is useful if you plan to bake a lot of cookies that will require embellishment with decorator's icing.

2. A parchment or wax paper cone is easy to make and disposable. Small parchment paper cones are now available in many stores selling kitchen equipment.

To make a paper cone: Cut a piece of parchment or wax paper into a square. Fold it in half diagonally to form a triangle. Holding the triangle, folded edge down, bring the lower right-hand corner up and curl it around so that it meets the inside top corner of the triangle, forming a cone. Next bring the lower left-hand corner up and wrap it around the outside of the cone so that it meets the outside top corner of the triangle. Fold the point where the three corners meet at the top of the cone down to the outside of the cone and tape it securely in place. Snip off a *tiny* piece from the bottom of the cone to make a hole through which the icing can be piped.

3. A plastic sandwich bag can be half-filled with icing and a tiny piece of the corner cut out, through which the icing can be piped.

Whichever method you use, take some time to practice and hone your decorating skills. The more adept and confident you are, the more creative you'll become. However, even a wavering line of icing outlining the branches of a Christmas tree cookie has a certain charm, so don't let lack of experience inhibit you.

FLAVORED SUGARS

Cinnamon sugar, vanilla sugar, and vanilla confectioners' sugar can be dusted over cookies, or the cookies can be dipped into the perfumed sugar. All three are quickly made and can be stored indefinitely.

OTHER DECORATIONS

White and colored sugar crystals, chocolate and colored shot, silver dragées, red hots, chocolate-covered coffee beans, currants, and even small candies can all be used to decorate Christmas cookies. However, we do not use any of the gummy, tasteless (in both senses of that word), and chemically toxic candied fruits, including citrus peel and red and green cherries, that are to be found in supermarkets beginning at Thanksgiving or earlier every year.

·

The recipes that follow are for the basic glazes, icings, and flavored sugars. We include as well recipes for homemade candied citrus peel, which is so delicious that it can be prettily packed and given by itself.

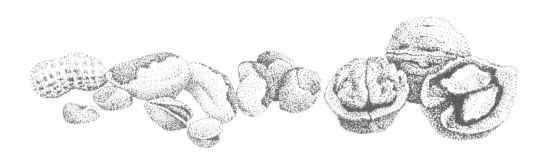

CONFECTIONERS' SUGAR GLAZE

ENOUGH TO GLAZE 50 TO 60 COOKIES

∎

¼ cup confectioners' sugar
1 tablespoon water

This is our building block recipe for a basic glaze. For a detailed description of how to flavor and use confectioners' sugar glazes see page 113.

Place the sugar in a bowl and whisk in the water until the glaze is smooth. Add more water, drop by drop, as necessary to achieve the consistency you want.

LEMON GLAZE

Substitute 1 tablespoon fresh lemon juice for the water.

ORANGE GLAZE

Substitute 1 tablespoon good-quality orange liqueur or fresh orange juice for the water.

ARMAGNAC GLAZE

ENOUGH TO GLAZE 50 TO 60 COOKIES

∎

¼ cup confectioners' sugar
1 tablespoon Armagnac

This glaze is best used on plain cookies. It adds a subtle, haunting flavor that in no way overpowers the simple goodness of the cookie. Best-quality brandy or cognac can be substituted for the Armagnac.

Place the sugar in a bowl and whisk in the Armagnac until the glaze is smooth. Add drops of water to thin out the glaze, if necessary.

DECORATOR'S ICING

ENOUGH TO DECORATE 50 OR 60 COOKIES

¼ cup egg whites, at room
   temperature
2¾ cups sifted confectioners'
   sugar, plus additional to make
   a stiff icing

This very simple icing is used to decorate lebkuchen (page 98) and pepparkakor cookies (page 102). It's thicker than the glazes and should be applied when the cookies have cooled.

In a large bowl, beat the egg whites with the confectioners' sugar until the mixture is smooth and stiff. Add a tablespoon or so of additional confectioners' sugar if the icing does not seem stiff enough to hold its shape when piped. Cover the icing with a damp dish towel to keep it from drying out and hardening as you use it.

This icing can be divided into small batches and colored with drops of food coloring as desired. To decorate cookies, fit a pastry bag with a small writing tip, fill the bag with frosting, and pipe frosting onto the cookies decoratively. Let the frosting dry before storing or hanging cookies. For ornaments, you might want to try decorating both sides of the cookie. Wait for the icing on one side to dry before icing the other side.

LEMON EGG WHITE GLAZE

MAKES 2 CUPS GLAZE

1 egg white, slightly beaten
1 tablespoon fresh lemon juice
1 teaspoon grated lemon zest
Pinch of salt
1½ cups confectioners' sugar

This variation on decorator's icing has a tangy lemon flavor that tastes especially good on spicy cookies, such as pepparkakor or pfeffernüsse.

Place all ingredients in a bowl and whisk until smooth. Add drops of water or lemon juice if the glaze is too thick.

CHOCOLATE GLAZE

ENOUGH TO GLAZE 35 TO 40 COOKIES

1 ounce unsweetened chocolate
1 ounce semisweet chocolate
¼ teaspoon vegetable shortening

This is a good decorative glaze for drizzling over plain spritz cookies—the unsweetened chocolate prevents it from being too cloying.

Melt the chocolates and shortening in the top of a double boiler over slowly simmering water, stirring often. Using a spoon, drizzle the glaze sparingly over cookies.

CHOCOLATE DIPPING GLAZE

ENOUGH TO DIP 60 COOKIES

8 ounces bittersweet or semisweet
    chocolate (perferably
    imported)
1 tablespoon vegetable shortening

A good-quality chocolate is crucial to the success of this glaze.

In the top of a double boiler, melt the chocolate and shortening over gently simmering water, stirring often. Remove the top of the double boiler from the bottom and place on a towel. Dip a part of each cookie in the chocolate, then scrape the bottoms of the cookies along the top of the pot to remove the excess chocolate. Place the cookies on wax paper for about 1 hour to allow the chocolate to harden.

Vanilla Sugar

MAKES 3 CUPS

∙

3 cups granulated sugar
1 vanilla bean, cut into 1-inch
    segments

This is wonderful for sprinkling on plain sugar cookies or butter cookies.

Place the sugar and the vanilla bean in a food processor fitted with the steel blade and process for 2 or 3 minutes, or until the vanilla bean is ground. (There will still be black specks visible in the sugar.) Transfer the vanilla sugar to an airtight container and let stand for 1 week. Sift the sugar before using. Store indefinitely.

Vanilla Confectioners' Sugar

MAKES 2 CUPS

∙

2 cups confectioners' sugar
1 vanilla bean, cut into segments

Vanilla beans are available in supermarkets, specialty food stores, and health food stores. Tahitian vanilla is deliciously aromatic.

Place the sugar and vanilla bean in the bowl of a food processor fitted with the steel blade and process until the vanilla bean is very finely chopped. Transfer the mixture to an airtight container and let stand for 1 week. Sift the sugar before using. Store indefinitely.

CINNAMON SUGAR

MAKES 1 CUP

·

1 cup granulated sugar
4 teaspoons cinnamon

It's impossible to imagine making Christmas cookies without cinnamon sugar.

Combine the sugar and cinnamon in a jar, cover, and shake. Store indefinitely.

CANDIED ORANGE AND LEMON PEEL

MAKES ABOUT 2 QUARTS

·

10 medium-sized unblemished
  oranges
6 large lemons
4 cups sugar
1⅔ cups water
Sugar for coating candied peel

Soft, juicy candied citrus peel is a special treat at any time of the year, and it's one of our favorite confections. Although the preparation is time-consuming, you'll find the time well spent because you'll end up with a considerable quantity of candied peel, which can be served, plain or dipped in chocolate glaze, as an after-dinner treat or used in other dessert recipes. The peel can be stored for months. For best results, select brightly colored, firm-skinned, unblemished fruit.

Cut the oranges and lemons into lengthwise quarters. Remove the flesh from each quarter in one piece, reserving it for another use, and place the peels in a large bowl of cold water. Using the edge of a teaspoon, scrape out and discard the weblike membrane from the inside of the peels, but leave most of the white pith attached to the outer layer of skin. (The cold water will help soften the membrane, making it easier to scrape out.)

Cut the peel on the bias into ¼-inch strips and place them in a saucepan. Add cold water to cover and bring to a boil over high heat. Drain the peel, rinse under cold running water, and drain again. Repeat the boiling, draining, and rinsing process three times more, allowing the peel to boil for 10 minutes after it has come to a boil for the final time.

Drain, rinse, and drain the peel once again, then place it in a large heavy saucepan with the 4 cups of sugar and the 1⅔ cups of water. Bring the mixture to a slow boil and cook slowly, stirring occasionally, until the peel is very soft and tender and has absorbed most of the syrup, about 1 hour. Every now and then, wash down the sides of the pan with a brush dipped in cold water or with a paper towel that has been dipped into cold water. Do not try to speed up the cooking process by raising the heat and boiling the syrup rapidly; to do so will insure the formation of sugar crystals and will harden and toughen the peel.

When it is cooked and tender, drain the peel, spread it out on a wax paper–lined baking sheet, and dry it overnight. Pour a cup or so of sugar into a paper or plastic bag and add small amounts of peel, tossing to coat the pieces with sugar. Repeat until all peel is coated. Store in airtight containers for up to 6 months.

CANDIED GRAPEFRUIT PEEL

Substitute 4 large thick-skinned grapefruit for the oranges and lemons. Leave just a scant ¼ inch of white pith attached to the rind. Boil, drain, and rinse the grapefruit peel six times in all, boiling it for 10 minutes the final time. Use the same amount of sugar called for in the first recipe.

COOKIES TO GO

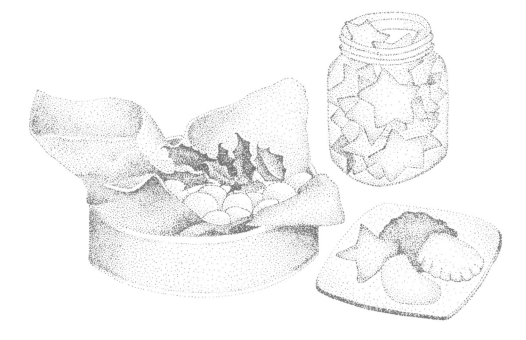

We like baking Christmas cookies because we love eating them, and next to that we like giving them away. Cookies are never the wrong gift, and you'll be able to take care of a lot of people on your gift list simply with a package of your favorite cookies.

A gift of cookies can be as simple as a dozen vanilla crescents nestled in a box lined with colored tissue paper or as elaborate as an old-fashioned cookie jar filled to the brim with dozens of your favorite cookies.

The secret to enjoying your holiday baking is to have a plan before you begin to bake, and to keep it simple.

PLANNING YOUR COOKIE MENU

You can turn out many batches of one kind of cookie, or you can bake a smorgasbord of cookies. What should you bake? We like variety, so we usually choose cookies of different flavors and shapes to package together. We start with three recipes as the basis for a cookie menu and then build on it if we're feeling more ambitious. Sometimes, though, we like variations on a theme, so we'll bake several different icebox or pressed cookies and fill a basket with just those. Why not try rolling out three different doughs and cutting them all out with one shape? A tin of stars or lions or gingerbread people in different flavors and colors can look quite striking. Use your imagination, and most of all, have fun!

Some of our favorite cookie menus are scattered throughout the book, and of course you can devise your own combinations.

PACKAGING YOUR COOKIES

Three or four batches of cookies will go a long way. Quantity is not the aim: Keep your containers small, unless you're giving cookies to a family with ten kids. What matters is that the cookies look delectable and the packaging appealing.

Almost anything, from a plastic bag to a fancy paper plate, from a wooden berry box saved from the summer to an antique platter, can become a container for cookies. One of the easiest ways to package cookies is to cut a piece of cardboard into a size and shape that will fit into the bottom of a one-gallon plastic food storage bag. Cover the cardboard with aluminum or colored foil and place it in the bottom of the bag. Arrange cookies on top of it, filling the bag with as many as you wish, then gather the top of the bag together and tie it closed with a large, colorful ribbon.

Label your gift with a card, perhaps one recycled from a Christmas past. Open the card, cut it in half, and discard the part with the printed message. Use the illustrated part of the card for your gift label, writing your greeting on either side of it.

These items are relatively inexpensive and look great filled with cookies:

Pretty paper or plastic plates. Fill them with cookies, slip a plastic food storage bag over the plate, tie with a ribbon.

Bakery boxes. Ask your local bakery or deli if you can buy a dozen or so of their small bakery boxes. They'll be inexpensive, and all you'll have to do is assemble them and line them with colored tissue.

Decorative paper bags. Line them with colored tissue paper, tuck cookies inside, and tie closed.

Baskets of all sizes and shapes. You can often find inexpensive small baskets, which are a perfect size for cookies, in import and discount stores.

Straw paper plate holders.

Wooden berry boxes.

China or glass plates. Wonderful sources for single plates are thrift shops, flea markets, garage sales, and the like. Those 25-cent one-of-a-kind plates "nobody" wants make lovely and ideal gift platters.

Plastic flower pots. Most gardeners have wondered what to do with all those empty green plastic pots that remain after the plants are in the ground. Cleaned up, lined with red or white tissue paper, and tied with a wide ribbon, they look very Christmassy.

Cloth napkins or dish towels with Christmas motifs or colors. You can find such items priced at next to nothing the week or two after Christmas. Place a plastic food storage bag filled with cookies in the center, draw up the ends, and tie with ribbon.

These containers are gifts in themselves:
Cookie jars, wide-mouthed glass canisters.
Metal canisters.
Decorative tins, those made for tea, crackers, fruits, and nuts, as well as baked goods. Look for them at garage sales and flea markets.
Glass or pottery bowls.
Bakeware. Springform pans, bundt pans, muffin tins, and even baking sheets can be filled with cookies.
Wooden cutting boards. Arrange cookies on top of a small cutting board and enclose cookies and cutting board inside a plastic food storage bag.
Old tinware molds, bread pans, sifters, colanders, and so on that you often find at garage sales can be lined with colored tissue and filled with cookies.

If all else fails:
Use other people's gift packaging. If you're a last-minute baker (as we were the year we were writing this book), by the time you've completed your Christmas baking, you may be the happy recipient of other people's baked goods, sent to you in attractive packages that may be just right for *your* cookies. Don't hesitate to use those pretty baskets; just be careful they're not returned to their original sender.

COOKIES TO TRAVEL

If you are shipping cookies, here's how to ensure that they reach their destination without crumbling. Cut parchment or tissue paper into 5- or 6-inch squares. Place 2 of the same kind of cookie back-to-back and wrap each pair individually in one of the squares.

Pack the wrapped cookies snugly but not too tightly in a rigid container, and fill empty spaces with nuts, shelled or not, popcorn, or crumpled pieces of tissue paper.

JUDY KNIPE is an artist and cookbook writer and editor. In addition to *The Christmas Cookie Book*, she has written, with Edward J. Safdie, *Spa Food* and *New Spa Food*. She divides her time between New York City and Vermont, where the inspiration for many of these cookies was born.

BARBARA MARKS is an avid cook, baker, and graphic designer whose design studio is in Connecticut. During the course of her career she has designed many cookbooks. *The Christmas Cookie Book* is the first she has also written.